Praise for *Fit to Lead*

The Proven 8-Week Solution for Shaping Up Your Body, Your Mind, and Your Career

---

"The information in this book can help you
gain an advantage in achieving your goals,
because the more fit you are, the better chance
you have to win in the game of life."

"Fabulous book! I'm truly impressed by the
straight-to-the-point information that helps
sift through all the diet and nutrition myths.
I would recommend *Fit to Lead* to all executives or
anyone with a busy schedule. Clearly, this book
offers the right ideas for becoming fit, staying
healthy, having more energy... all of which
create better productivity!"

"Reading *Fit to Lead* won't do a damn thing for you.
Read and follow it, and you will take control of
your life, both physically and mentally forever."

"There's no doubt about it. The more fit I am, the more productive I am. If I'm exercising regularly and eating right, then I can better handle the stressors that I have to face every day as a busy executive. *Fit to Lead* truly contains a detailed program to help me achieve the optimal level of fitness necessary to be a top performer."

—Charles J. Barnard, senior vice president,
southwest regional director,
Corporate Real Estate, Bank of America

"Finally, here's a book that acknowledges the vital link between fitness and leadership. *Fit to Lead* is a must-read for leaders of all organizations, and at all levels, from the mail room to the executive suite. The insights and practical advice provided are sure to improve the quality of life not only for every reader but also for the organizations they lead."

—Robert F. Ashcraft, director and associate professor,
Center for Nonprofit Leadership and Management,
Arizona State University

Fit to Lead

Fit to Lead

The Proven 8-Week Solution for Shaping Up
Your Body, Your Mind, and Your Career

Christopher P. Neck, Ph.D.
Tedd L. Mitchell, M.D.
Charles C. Manz, Ph.D.
Emmet C. Thompson II, D.S.L.

Foreword by Kenneth H. Cooper, M.D., M.P.H.,
"The Father of Aerobics" and author of *Faith-Based Fitness*

St. Martin's Press New York

www.stmartins.com

Library of Congress Cataloging-in-Publication Data

Fit to lead : the proven 8-week solution for shaping up your body, your mind, and your career / Christopher P. Neck... [et al.] ; foreword by Kennth H. Cooper.—1st U.S. ed.
    p. cm.
    ISBN 0-312-32537-1
    EAN 978-0312-32537-4
    1. Physical fitness. 2. Executives—Health and hygiene. I. Neck, Christopher P.
    GV481.F545 2004
    613.7'1—dc22

                                      2003026388

First Edition: May 2004

10 9 8 7 6 5 4 3 2 1

To our wives:
Jennifer, Janet, Karen, and Teresa

Contents

Part I

Chapter One

Why Should You Get Fit?

Chapter Two

The Fit to Lead Prescription

Chapter Three

No More Excuses

Chapter Four

Eating for Fitness

Chapter Five

Fit from the Inside Out

Part II

Acknowledgments

Our author team has been fortunate to be touched by many people who have influenced us directly or indirectly and thus helped us discover, shape, and develop the material in *Fit to Lead*. In particular, we would like to thank Dr. Kenneth H. Cooper for his unconditional support of this manuscript and his invaluable assistance as well as other members of the Cooper Clinic, including Mariann Lousteau and Cynthia Grantham for their time and efforts. Our team would also like to acknowledge Connie Tyne of the Cooper Wellness Program for supporting us and believing in the book.

We'd like to offer a special thank-you to David W. Manz, who provided very helpful input at key points of the development process. Special thanks also goes to Alisa Bauman for her magical editing touches during various stages of the book.

Next, we would like to recognize Virginia Tech (especially the Pamplin College of Business), the University of Massachusetts at Amherst (especially the Isenberg School of Management), and Regent University. Our thanks extend to our deans, chairs, and special colleagues: Richard Sorensen, Rich Wokutch, and Jon Shepard (Virginia Tech); Tom O'Brien, Bill Wooldridge (University of Massachusetts); and Bruce Winston and Jacque King (Regent University). Additionally, Charles C. Manz truly thanks the generosity of Charles and Janet Nirenberg, who funded the Nirenberg Chair of Business Leadership, the position he holds at the University of Massachusetts.

In addition, we want to express our appreciation to the St. Martins Press team for their very able assistance in converting our ideas into a book. We want especially to thank Marian Lizzi, Julie Mente, Heather Jackson, and Elizabeth Bewley for their above-and-beyond support in making this book a reality.

We also want to thank the many individuals who have supported us and who have had a special impact on our thinking about fitness and/or leadership, including Kathi Lovelace, Hank Sims, Greg Stewart, Vikas Anand, Peter Hom, Bob Marx, Brent Neck, Heidi Neck, Stuart Mease, Chuck Koerber, Krishna Kumar, Jeff Houghton, Mike Goldsby, Richard Hackman, Chris Argyris, Ed Lawler, Fred Luthans, Ted Levitt, John Kotter, Craig Pearce, Karen Manz, Denny Gioia, Kim Cameron, Carl Fey, Robert Ashcraft, Joe Patin, David Colvin, Art Bedeian, Bob Geiman, Tom Collingwood, and our many other colleagues, too numerous to name here.

Finally, Christopher P. Neck would like to say thank you to Dick Heinrich for being the catalyst for Neck's initial meeting with Dr. Cooper in 1996. Without this meeting, the book *Fit to Lead* may have never happened.

Foreword

When my first book, *Aerobics,* was published in 1968, I never dreamed it would have the worldwide impact that it did. As an Air Force officer, I had studied exercise in the hopes of developing a program for military personnel. What started out as an interest in exercise physiology became a lifelong journey of discovery. Some exercise concepts developed in the 1950s and 1960s proved to be improper, unnecessary, or downright unhealthy. My primary goal became bridging the gap in exercise between faddism and scientific legitimacy. In order to accomplish this, however, I had a lot to do. For starters, I had to practice what I preached. I knew what it was like to be out of shape, because I had been there. Although I had been an athlete in high school and college, the rigors of medical school and training had eventually displaced exercise and healthy eating from my daily routine. Like others who find themselves in such a position, I gained weight, lost energy, and felt the impact on my quality of life. I took the bull by the horns. I put myself back on a routine of regular activity and good nutrition, and before long I was training for my first Boston Marathon. The rest, as they say, is history.

Second, I knew I had to prove to others, beyond a shadow of a doubt, that being physically fit is a key ingredient to living a healthy life. To accomplish this, I established the Cooper Institute for Aerobics Research in 1970, hired the appropriate staff, and began collecting data on patients I saw at the Cooper Clinic. Over the past thirty-three years, we have grown from a small "mom and pop" organization to a leading researcher in the field of exercise and health. The Aerobics Center Longitudinal Database, located on our campus, currently houses more information on fitness and health than any databank in the world. Researchers from all over come to study at our center, and landmark articles continue to come from this extensive databank. I'm proud of the work done by my staff of dedicated researchers, doctors, nurses, exercise physiologists, and support staff. As a young physician, I never dreamed this to be possible, but looking back on the past forty years, I take great pride in the things that have been accomplished. The Aerobics Center continues to be the "gold standard" in the health and fitness industry. We have quite literally changed the way the world thinks about exercise, nutrition, and healthy living. Gone are the days when a lonely jogger gets funny looks. Instead, today we see throngs of people crowding streets for events celebrating physical activity, busy executives hitting the gym, and employees taking walking and stretching breaks.

Making people aware of the benefits of physical fitness is not enough. I would daresay that no one in our country is unaware of the benefits of exercise. In spite of this, 60 percent of adult Americans follow no form of regular exercise! Worse still is the fact that the rate of obesity among our children has tripled in just over a decade. While many have embraced our concepts, many others have not. As a nation, we face a crisis if we don't address our collective habits. In addition to diminished quality of life, health-care costs will surely increase, and productivity will suffer. In short, while we've made great strides, there's a lot more to do.

Based on our latest data, the good news is that physical fitness doesn't require Herculean efforts. Our research suggests that consistent, moderate exercise is the key to success. When I first started, the approach was "if you walk, jog; if you jog, run; if you run, run harder!" You get the picture. The more the better. Research has shown us, however, that this is not necessary. Huge benefits can result by simply making consistent activity a part of your life. And the benefits aren't just physical. I've been privileged to work with many executives, politicians, celebrities, and other professionals in my career. I have been struck by how many of them, in spite of hectic schedules, have made exercise and good nutrition a priority. By dedicating themselves to healthy habits, I have seen them become healthier people and more effective leaders. When patients tell me that they don't have time to exercise, I point out that being fit will make them more energetic and productive—in a word, more effective. In turn, this will actually allow them to accomplish much more each day. *Fit to Lead* drives this point home. It offers reasonable prescriptions based on the best knowledge available for helping busy leaders become healthier and more effective.

As this book makes clear, our approach at the Cooper Clinic is not about developing iron men. Rather, it's about improving lives. By reading about executive fitness in *Fit to Lead*, you are opening a life-changing door to better health and greater effectiveness at work. If you want to get more out of life and lead others to do the same, I recommend that you read this book.

—*Kenneth H. Cooper, M.D., M.P.H.*

Meeting the Challenge
of Being Fit to Lead

Physical fitness is the basis for all other forms of excellence.

—John F. Kennedy

Are more fit leaders better leaders? Before you answer, consider the following scenario.

A senior executive of a Fortune 100 company (perhaps it's you), after only five hours of sleep, arrives at her office very early. Numerous meetings and phone calls later, she realizes that it's already two P.M. *and she has not eaten anything since an early breakfast of coffee and donuts.*

She heads out the door to grab some lunch. As she walks to the restaurant, she recalls her days as a runner a few years back and how good it felt to be in shape. Now, given her busy schedule, she rarely exercises. Halfway to the restaurant, she notices a group of runners approaching at a brisk pace. She thinks she recognizes a fit-looking middle-aged man. "Who is he—he looks so familiar, and how does he find the time to fit in exercise in his day? He must be unemployed!" Then as they reach each other, he notices her stare and smiles at her. Her jaw drops as she finally realizes who he is.

Now it's time to play *Who Wants to be a Millionaire?* The middle-aged man in the scenario above is a:

(a) past Olympic runner

(b) professional triathlete

(c) fitness trainer

(d) well-recognized corporate CEO

What is your answer?

Are you ready?

Is this your final answer? The correct answer is d.

Surprisingly, at a time when most Americans find a plethora of reasons not to exercise, some of the busiest people in the country, people who arguably have the most frenetic and grueling schedules of anyone in the world, make fitness a top priority. In fact, current and former presidents, including George W. Bush, Bill Clinton, and Jimmy Carter, as well as former vice President Al Gore, exercised regularly. Running and physical fitness has almost become a prerequisite for a term in the Oval Office!

In addition to these "leaders of the free world," a growing number of CEOs and other business executives are putting fitness first in their lives.

The list of top-level executives who make fitness a priority reads like *Who's Who*. Consider these examples:

- Tom Monaghan, the founder of Domino's Pizza and current chairman of the Mater Christi Foundation, runs about four miles or uses the StairMaster every day. He also spends thirty minutes on the Nautilus machines, alternating upper and lower body every other day. When traveling he does push-ups and crunches along with running. He consumes about two thousand calories a day, and does not eat any desserts or sweets.

- James Harris, vice president of player personnel for the NFL's Jacksonville Jaguers, exercises three to four days per week. His regimen consists of twenty to thirty minutes on the treadmill or a brisk walk outdoors, some weight work, stretching, and bike riding. He avoids fried foods, red meat, and eating after seven P.M.

• Michael Mangum, president of the Mangum Group, performs some form of cardiovascular exercise such as running two hours per week, and he lifts weights two to three times a week. He also tries to minimize fat and cholesterol while maximizing fruit intake.

• Dina Gartland, a partner at age thirty-one at the geotechnical firm Leighton & Associates, is out of bed at five A.M. to train three hours as a triathlete before starting her long workday.

• Dr. Thomas Frist Jr., chairman and CEO of Columbia/HCA Healthcare, uses time between business flights to jog around airports or nearby cities.

• Charles O. Rossotti, commissioner of the Internal Revenue Service, jogs five miles a day.

• Julian C. Day, president and CEO of Kmart, runs half marathons and surfs.[1]

According to various surveys, many more executives are indeed placing a priority on their physical fitness. A survey of executives from the top three thousand U.S. companies (identified from Fortune 500, the Inc. 100, the Venture Fast Track 100, and Dun's List of Large and Small Companies) revealed that two-thirds of the executives exercised at least three times weekly, with more than 90 percent of that group using aerobic exercise as the cornerstone of their workouts. Also, more than 90 percent reported being careful about their diet, 81 percent had a complete physical exam within the previous two years, and only 10 percent of the executives smoked (compared with the national average of more than 25 percent).[2]

Why are so many extremely busy and powerful executives placing fitness at the top of their priorities list? Because regular exercise and healthy eating not only helps improve their health, it also bolsters their job performance—and ultimately their careers.

On-the-Job Fitness

We all hear about the health benefits of staying fit—the reduced incidence of heart disease, lower cancer risk, better weight control, and so on. But few people mention a rather compelling benefit, one that hits people right in their wallets and pocketbooks. The more fit you are, the better your likelihood of performing well on the job.

Fitness has serious positive benefits for executives, the companies they represent, and the employees who work for them. During the past thirty-two years, we've tracked the success of more than twenty-five thousand executives who have participated in Executive Lifestyle evaluations at the Cooper Clinic.

We've reviewed numerous studies about the mental, physical, emotional, and lifetime benefits of fitness for workers and executives. And we've interviewed key executives about the benefits of their fitness habits, including interviews with President George W. Bush.[3]

Our research shows that leaders who are fit are better able to handle the enormous demands that confront them, including endless meetings, grueling travel schedules, high pressure, and stress.

Perhaps not as obvious as the contribution to job performance or the other benefits mentioned, fitness also helps you live longer. The fitness of key executives can help determine the success of the company. An illness or death of a top executive could have far reaching consequences for an organization.

Fitting in Fitness

We all know how tough it is to motivate ourselves to exercise. Given our jobs, families, and other obligations, we can easily find reasons to talk ourselves out of going for that run or heading to the gym. And it's so much easier to grab that fast food than plan a healthy meal.

Yet, if George W. Bush—one of the busiest people in the world—can find the time to run, the rest of us can too. Given the president's discipline to stay fit, we wanted to know what motivates him to exercise most days of the week and to watch what he eats. Fortunately, finding the answer to this question wasn't as tough a challenge as it sounds. We're good friends with Kenneth Cooper, M.D., of the Cooper Aerobics Center in Dallas, Texas, who is George W. Bush's personal physician.

For President Bush, fitness starts with making a commitment. He disciplines himself to run three miles four days a week. He also uses the treadmill and elliptical trainer two days a week and lifts weights one or two days a week.

The president makes no excuses in terms of making time for fitness—regardless of what he is doing and where he is. George W. Bush credits running with making him a better leader. He says that working out makes him perform his duties better because it gives him time to think and more energy.

Let's revisit our opening question, "Are more fit leaders better leaders?" We argue yes, and President Bush and many other effective executives serve to support our contention. His is a common story among executives and employees—fitness makes him more effective.

Throughout *Fit to Lead*, you'll read more about the fitness efforts of many successful and influential executives. You'll find out exactly why they prioritize exercise, how they've benefited from it, and how they manage to fit it into their schedules. You'll read the complete story about how they became Fit to Lead.

And this can be your story, as well. You need only make a firm commitment to becoming Fit to Lead. Throughout the pages of this book, we'll provide all the tools you need to make your journey a success.

In Part I, you'll learn why we're so convinced that our Fit to Lead formula works. You'll read study after study that links improved fitness with better job performance. You'll hear from executives just like you who experienced huge on-the-job benefits from their fitness programs. And you'll find out why and how our three-pronged fitness formula will work for you.

You'll also discover the three crucial elements of your Fit to Lead program—regular exercise, healthy eating, and self-leadership. In other words, you'll learn to develop body fitness, nutritional fitness, and mental fitness.

These three Fit to Lead elements support and build on one another. Your nutritional program will create the energy you need for your exercise habits. Your self-leadership program will help you boost your motivation to stick to your exercise and eating plans.

Our exercise, nutrition, and self-leadership programs are based on years of research conducted by our author team. They've worked for countless executives, and they will work for you. We've designed them specifically for the fast-paced executive lifestyle. You can do the exercise routines anywhere, anytime—at three A.M. in a hotel room or at noon in your office. You can practice the nutrition recommendations wherever you eat, including fast-food restaurants. And our self-leadership techniques are based on sound business tips. They won't just help you stick to your exercise and eating plans. They will also help you improve your job performance!

Throughout this section, you'll receive tips from busy executives. They will reveal their secrets for fitting in fitness and healthy eating during eighty-hour workweeks, with hectic travel schedules, and numerous client dinners.

In Part II, you'll embark on your Total Life Makeover. You'll receive step-by-step advice for successfully incorporating the Fit to Lead principles into your life. With the Fit to Lead plan, you will never feel overwhelmed with tasks. We've broken the Total Life Makeover into small, easily attainable steps that you will tackle slowly over eight weeks. By the end of eight weeks, you will have overhauled your diet, your thinking habits, and your life. You will have become Fit to Lead. Most important, you'll have the tools to become fit for life.

And that's important. This isn't a get-fit-quick book. We recommend habits that you must stick to for a lifetime to achieve and maintain your success. But this won't feel difficult. Once you master the Fit to Lead concepts during your eight-week makeover, you'll have become fit from the inside out. You won't fall off the fitness wagon.

Finally, we'll also show you how to achieve what we call "SuperLeadership." To truly improve your company, your new fitness habits must go beyond just you. They must seep into the psyche of every employee at your company. We'll teach you how to do just that by giving you proven prescriptions for starting company fitness programs as well as for successfully encouraging fitness in those who work for you.

Improved fitness will make you a better leader, so let's get started.

Before embarking on any exercise and/or nutritional program, obtain medical clearance from a qualified physician.

Part I

Chapter One

Why Should You Get Fit?

More Energy, Less Stress, Improved
Job Performance, and Much, Much More[1]

*There's no question that people who are fit are more
productive. They enjoy their work more and accomplish more.*

—Dr. Jerome Zuckerman, exercise physiologist

Being a leader today is not for the meek, the timid, or the mild.
Being a leader is not easy! The job of the executive has become
more intense over the last decade. A profusion of new demands confronts executives, particularly physical ones.

For example, the global economic thrust of many businesses
today has forced CEOs to step up their travel schedules in an
attempt to develop and maintain an international presence for
their companies. In addition, simply being responsible for
many people, their welfare, and the success of the company
creates a stressful, physical demand. Endless meetings and extremely long workdays are now par for the course for executives.

Yet executives who enjoy optimal fitness—the ability to accomplish life's activities without undue fatigue—can better
handle these demands and thus perform better in their daily
tasks with more energy, focus, and creativity.

In short, fitness works. Fit executives perform better than

unfit ones. We know because we've reviewed numerous studies and tracked thousands of executives—fit and unfit—who come through the doors of the Cooper Clinic each year. We also interviewed numerous executives, and our research all adds up to one thing—an executive's worth can be tied directly to his or her fitness level.

For example, Michael Mangum is president and CEO of the Mangum Group, a diversified, closely held business with interests in highway construction, asphalt paving, and equipment management. The company employs more than 350 people and generates over $80 million in annual revenues. He told us:

> *I do believe fitness impacts my job. I usually exercise during the middle of the day, say, one to four P.M. or so. I find that my energy level is much enhanced when I return from a workout. Further, I find that because I choose to go during the day, my thoughts tend toward work while exercising. I have some of my most creative thoughts when working out.*

Judith Kaplan had a similar perspective while she served as CEO of Action Products International, Inc., an educational toy manufacturer in Orlando that generates $8.2 million in sales each year.

> *I never felt better, physically and mentally, than when I was exercising regularly three times a week. I could work harder. Instead of collapsing at the end of the day, I'd still feel good.*

Likewise, Tom Monaghan, the founder of Domino's Pizza and current chairman of the Mater Christi Foundation, a private foundation that focuses on Catholic education, Catholic media, community projects, and other Catholic charities, says:

> *Since I have been exercising regularly and eating right, I have had more energy and a better self-image. Fitness and exercise*

also have helped me develop good disciplinary habits, which carries over to good business habits.

James Harris, vice president of player personnel for the NFL's Jacksonville Jaguars, offers a similar perspective:

I believe fitness can enhance your concentration and endurance to perform the task at hand. Physical conditioning gives you confidence and energy to achieve.

Carol Cone, president of Cone Communications, a marketing and public relations firm, also believes that fitness enhances her on-the-job performance:

I must make fifty to one hundred decisions a day, and it's important to have the same clarity of thinking at seven or eight o'clock at night as at seven or eight o'clock in the morning.[2]

The Proof Is in the Research

Don't just take the words of a few successful executives and the president of the United States. Hundreds of well-controlled studies prove what they've learned from personal experience— that fitness improves job performance.

In one study, commercial real estate stockbrokers who participated in an aerobics-training program (walking and/or running once a day, three times a week, for twelve weeks) earned larger sales commissions than brokers who did not participate. Also, workers from a hospital equipment firm who participated in an aerobics-training program (walking, running, swimming, and/or bicycling once a day, four times a week, for twenty-four weeks) enjoyed greater productivity and job satisfaction than workers who did not participate.[3]

In addition, a variety of studies show that fitness boosts

mental performance, especially for individuals within the age range of many executives. For example, one study of fifty-six college professors revealed that physically active people process data faster and experience a slower age-related decline in information-processing speed than inactive people. Similarly, a study of postal workers found that not only younger employees (age eighteen to thirty) but also more fit older ones (forty-three to sixty-two) consistently outperformed less fit employees on mental tasks involving information processing.[4]

Individuals who are fit are also less likely to become obese and more likely to possess higher levels of energy and enjoy enhanced feelings of well-being.[5] Further studies have shown that fit individuals tend to enjoy psychological benefits as well, including a reduction in anxiety, depression, tension, and stress.[6]

EXECUTIVE ENLIGHTENMENT

"My weight has dropped twenty-five pounds, my body fat dropped from 19 percent to roughly 10 percent, and my cholesterol from 225 to 110," says Michael Mangum, two years after embarking on the Fit to Lead program. "My ultrafast CT scan showed no spread of previous heart-related calcifications, and my time on the treadmill stress test improved by three minutes or so. The program has made a big difference for me. On a related point, I find that I miss less time from work due to illness. Since I started on a pretty rigorous wellness program, I have seen a marked drop in my sick days. I virtually don't get sick any more."[7]

The Benefits Keep Adding Up

As we have been emphasizing, besides your job performance, fitness also improves your health. In fact, sticking to an exercise program may be the most important thing you can do to ensure a longer, fuller life.

For example, one study revealed improvements in cardiovascular function and strength, as well as reductions in body fat and weight, for sixty-six men engaged in a two-year exercise program located within their corporate headquarters. Another study, led by Dean Ornish, M.D., shows that lifestyle changes that include diet and exercise can reverse the atherosclerotic changes of coronary heart disease and unblock arteries enough to avoid surgery. Finally, an estimated 35 percent of cancers, the second leading cause of death in the United States, are related to diet.[8] In fact, there is a growing body of evidence that links poor food choices with the incidence of cancer, particularly cancer of the esophagus, breast, prostate, and colon.[9]

Additionally, solid evidence shows that physically fit people live longer. A recent study published in the *New England Journal of Medicine* of more than one million adults during a fourteen-year period confirmed that being overweight shortened a person's life.

Several landmark studies done at the Cooper Institute for Aerobics Research have investigated this association between fitness and death. One of these seminal research projects investigated the relationship between fitness levels and the risk of dying in more than ten thousand men and three thousand women. The study revealed that men and women with low levels of physical fitness had more than twice the mortality rate than those with even a moderate level of physical fitness. Fitness in this case helped reduce risk for all causes of mortality, including diabetes, cancer, and heart disease.[10]

The major finding from this study and others—that physical fitness can prolong one's life—has tremendous significance for you and the organization you lead. Your fitness level can greatly impact the success of your company. If you become ill, especially if you're a top-level executive, your ill health could pose far-reaching consequences for your organization.[11] Al Hirsch, president of G+A Communications, learned this lesson all too well in 1991, when he was diagnosed with a heart fibrillation. He remarked:

> *Maybe it was stress, maybe it was poor diet. I don't know the exact cause—the doctors don't either—but I knew I had to start eating right, exercising right, and somehow handle the anxiety that comes with managing a business.*[12]

Lean foods and a twenty-minute run four times a week remedied Hirsch's heart problem. A fitness program focusing on exercise and diet helped him gain optimal health.

Fitness is important not only to you but also to the economic health of the company you run. Economic effects from cardiovascular disease (which research shows can be related to poor fitness habits) amounted to an estimated $286.5 billion in 1999.[13] According to the U.S. Department of Health and Human Services, such losses affect employer and employee alike "in lost work days and wages, lost productivity, increased health care costs, and lowered morale."[14]

Bob Jeffrey, president of the North American Region of the $4 billion grossing J. Walter Thompson advertising agency, recognizes the benefits of fitness for employees in his organization. His employees can "work out and relax in a 'de-stress room,' get free massages and yoga or nutrition lessons, join a company sports team, and consult with a personal trainer." As Mr. Jeffrey remarks: "We're [the company] totally dependent on the ideas and talent of our people, so we have to help them feel great about themselves."[15]

Fitness Designed for Your Needs

So now you know why you need to get in shape. Let's move on to how.

Based on research conducted by the Cooper Institute for Aerobics Research and other scholars, the Fit to Lead program offers you a three-pronged approach to fitness. You'll find sound prescriptions for exercise and diet, as well as a leadership plan that will help you to better implement these prescriptions into your life.[15] We've specifically designed all three components for busy executives.

The Fit to Lead prescriptions will help you achieve optimal levels of fitness necessary for superior leadership performance, giving you the tools to begin a Fit to Lead lifestyle. In Chapter 2, we share more details about this exciting program that offers the potential to change your life and career!

Chapter Two

The Fit to Lead Prescription

Our Three-Part Program Will Get You Fit from the Inside Out— Helping You to Become Fit for Life[1]

> *Knowledge cannot make us all leaders, but it can help us decide which leader to follow.*
>
> —*Management Digest*

Now you're convinced that becoming Fit to Lead will help you improve your job performance. Here's the big question: How can you get there?

The science of fitness and nutrition can seem confusing, mostly because so many programs offer divergent approaches. From the latest fad diet books to locker room chat, misinformation abounds. So now that you're convinced that you want to get fit, we will convince you that the Fit to Lead program is the best way for you to get there.

Everyone wants to change from flabby to fit fast, and busy executives are no exception. Millions of people are hooked on the latest ticket to quick-and-easy weight reduction: melt-away-fat belts, exercise programs without exercise, high-protein diets, no-fat diets, low-sugar diets, and even high-carbohydrate diets.

Unlike such fad diets, we don't promise miracles. Yes, you will probably lose weight, if that's you're goal. You will gain more energy. Your outlook on life will improve. Most important, your job performance will perk up.

But you won't transform yourself overnight, in one week, or even in one month.

Every fitness fad promises that the pounds will slip off in record time, results will appear almost instantaneously. What these fads don't tell you is that your chances of *keeping off those pounds and staying fit* are close to zero. Studies show that five years after beginning a diet without an exercise component, the vast majority of the dieters have gained back the weight they lost—and more. The big problem is compliance: Most programs, particularly those that require you to give up major food groups, are just too darn hard to follow day in and day out for an extended period of time.

Once the weight comes off, the dieter thinks he or she is home free and then proceeds to gobble up previously "banned substances" such as cookies, potatoes, breads, or fats. Before long, the pounds creep back on, the bad habits take over, and the dieter and diet fail.

But there's another problem with diets. They focus on only one aspect of the equation—food. We've found that you need a three-pronged attack on flab, one that includes exercise, nutrition, and mental toughness. Skip any component and you risk failure.

A Fit to Lead lifestyle plan is NOT a fad. It's also NOT a diet.

In our plan, there are no taboo foods, no slick promises of instant weight loss, and no complicated balancing act to achieve success. Instead, you'll find a simple three-pronged approach that every executive can follow.

Not only are you allowed to be "bad" some of the time, but you are actually encouraged to do so. Under this plan you follow a "workweek" mind-set. From Monday through Friday you follow good, healthy principles of nutrition and exercise, which over the long haul will help you lose weight and get fit systematically—and permanently. Then, on the weekends, you get a chance to splurge *a little*. In other words, eat right and exercise the majority of the time and you earn the right to have the occasional feast on the weekend and lie on the couch and watch television.

The plan includes the following three components, all specifically designed for an executive's busy lifestyle.

1. **Body Fitness.** Our exercise plan requires no fancy equipment. You can do it anywhere, anytime—including your office, hotel room, or living room. The exercise program will help you improve three fitness variables: your endurance, your strength, and your flexibility. (You'll learn more about how each of those variables will improve your job performance in Chapter 3.) This is an excuse-proof exercise program. We've tested it on numerous executives. It works.

2. **Nutritional Fitness.** We know that executives lead busy lifestyles. We know you often eat out at restaurants, including fast-food ones. We know you often must grab food on the go. Finally, we know that you may have very little time to shop for and prepare healthy food. That's why we designed our nutrition plan in Chapter 4 around your unique needs and lifestyle. You'll learn how to make more healthful food choices no matter where you eat, including fast-food and airport restaurants. With this eight-step nutritional plan, you can't go wrong.

3. **Mental Fitness.** Our eight-step self-leadership plan uses sound business principles and applies them to eating and exercising. You'll learn how to lead yourself toward sound body and nutritional fitness. Exercise and healthful eating will become an automatic and even

enjoyable habit. It's what sets our program apart from other fitness and weight-loss programs. And it's what will help you get and remain fit for the rest of your life.

Does this all sound too good to be true?

It's for real. It works. We know, because we have seen the benefits of this program for years. It's worked for the countless numbers of executives who have come to the Cooper Clinic for lifestyle advice.

In fact, one member of our author team, Tedd Mitchell, would like to share how the Fit to Lead plan impacted him personally. What follows is a story of his wife and himself and how Fit to Lead hit home for both.

The Bare Midriff Blues

Dr. Janet Tornelli had a dirty little secret. She never, ever wore two-piece bathing suits or belly-baring workout clothes for fear of showing off her midriff.

It wasn't that she was not beautiful. From the time we met in medical school, I was smitten. She was tall and athletic, with black hair and fiery brown eyes that hinted at her Italian-American roots. Her vivacious personality owed much to the Latin culture that she adopted as a child growing up in Mexico City. And she was smart, real smart. She was the kind of woman who was destined for success as an executive. At age twenty-two, she could match me mile for mile as we jogged around town and forkful for forkful as we ate our hearts out at the local dives. She worked out five days a week, taught aerobics twice weekly, and ran up to five miles on the other days.

But through all the high-impact exercise, through all the sweat and effort, she always stayed discreetly covered up. Her workout clothes were always layered. Bathing suits always had to be one piece.

"I never had a figure I was happy with," she confessed.

After we got married and started to have kids, her routine—and her figure—began to change. With each birth, Janet put on a couple of pounds that never all came off. She gained fifty-five pounds with our first child, which she lost by drinking a low-calorie shake at breakfast and lunch and eating a very light dinner. By the time our third child arrived, she had gained a total of ten extra pounds that stayed.

The demands of juggling three kids on top of starting a busy medical practice left less time for workouts. What's more, she thought she was eating the right things: low-fat Pop-Tarts while on the way to work, Diet Cokes during the day—you get the picture. Business lunches and dinners were regular events, and weekends with the family provided a virtual smorgasbord of goodies that she found hard to refuse—and control. By the time she hit age thirty-three, Janet had gained a total of fifteen extra pounds, and her weight was fast moving into a range that we deemed "unacceptable" at the Cooper Clinic.

I know, because I got to break the bad news to her.

Janet had just joined the Cooper Clinic as its first female physician and I had been eager to show her the ropes. To give her a feel for how things were done at a preventive medicine clinic, I thought the best approach was to treat her like a patient and do her pre-employment physical. I took off my husband hat, put on my doctor hat, and gave her a rundown of her physical condition, based on the Cooper Clinic's extensive battery of standard tests.

At the end of the morning Janet had been through a number of tests, including body-fat studies, and the results were in front of me in a thick folder. As we sat facing each other in my office, it was time to present the facts.

"According to test results, to get to an acceptable weight for a woman your age, you've got to lose twelve pounds. To get to an ideal weight you've got to lose fifteen. That's what the Cooper Clinic says is an 'athletic' weight."

For a few minutes Janet didn't say a word. She just sat there staring at me. Then she got mad. Real mad.

"You're crazy!" she said. "I can't lose that much weight. Fifteen pounds, no way!"

Instead of responding, I simply forged ahead with an explanation of her other test results, and she quickly got back to business. By the time I closed her medical file and walked her to the door, she was as crisp and efficient as her white coat.

"See you at home," she said. She wasn't smiling.

I knew better than to take it personally. The truth was that Janet was disgusted with herself. She's the kind of physician and leader who can't tell anyone to do something she hasn't done herself. As a doctor, she had once taken a diuretic just to see how it made patients feel. Under the circumstances, how could she tell patients, "You have to lose weight," if her own weight was questionable?

The minute she got home, Janet took a close look at her diet and realized that her eating habits were in shambles. For years, she had been eating those low-fat Pop-Tarts, low-fat cookies, and low-fat desserts of all kinds, assuming that if the label said "low-fat" or "no-fat," the calories wouldn't add up. But the truth was, cookie for cookie, she was eating almost the same number or calories in a low-fat product as she would in a regular one.

Within days of her Cooper Clinic exam, she had made a decision to turn around her eating and exercise regimen. She quit buying low-fat pastries. She went off caffeine, including diet sodas, and kicked up her exercise routine to five days per week. Additionally, she increased the length of her daily exercise routine to forty minutes.

Finally, she took the boldest and, as it turned out for both of us, most revolutionary step of all: She made a commitment to cut calories during the week and treat herself to splurges only on the weekends. Five days a week, she emphasized good, lean proteins, fruits, and vegetables. No in-between meals or late-night snacking. Lots of water throughout the day. And no junk food. We continue to eat out on Friday and Saturday nights, and she doesn't hesitate to order a hamburger if she wants one. However, when she splurges, she never gorges, and she makes choices that are healthier and lower calorie than before. When in the past she would have *loaded up on the fries, she would now happily choose to eat a salad instead.*

Within the first month, she had started shedding pounds. By the end of the third month she had lost ten pounds and lowered her body fat significantly. Within six months, her body fat had dropped to 19 percent of her total body weight.

Even more important to her, she began to understand that she could maintain this program over the long term. "This is something I can do the rest of my life," she said.

These days, when summer rolls around and it's time for a new bathing suit, she heads straight for the two-piece rack. And after a day's work at the Cooper Clinic, she heads to the fitness center. You can easily spot Janet. She's the one on the elliptical trainer—with the bare midriff!

Janet's decision to embark on the Fit to Lead program has transformed her family. These days when Tedd comes home from work, he grabs a handful of raw carrots and a big glass of water instead of a soda. On the weekends, however, he does not hold back. On Saturday morning, he heads for the doughnut shop and does not feel guilty. There is no guilt because the doughnuts are an exception, not the rule to his eating habits! He also knows that his regular exercise helps burn off the extra calories.

A Fit to Lead lifestyle should become so ingrained that you eventually don't have to think about it. Executives in positions of authority are role models, whether you like it or not. As Janet realized, you can't tell others to do something you are not doing yourself. You shouldn't have to resort to tricks or dietary gymnastics. You simply need to develop a program that you can stick to over the long term, and the balance in your eating and exercise habits will come naturally.

This is not some newfangled fad. Instead, a Fit to Lead lifestyle emphasizes scientifically established principles of healthy eating and exercise.

As a leader, you must learn to make eating and exercise

choices that are right for you and your lifestyle. In spite of hectic schedules, travel, and other time commitments, you choose what you eat. You choose when to splurge. You choose when you have reached the weight you are happy with. You choose when to move, and you choose when to rest.

Remember that it's "Okay to be bad." If you commit yourself to a "workweek mind-set," you have a green light to splurge some on the weekends. Attempting to deprive yourself of favorite foods for a lifetime and stick to an exercise-every-single-day-without-a-break regimen is what dooms most people from the beginning. If someone says to us, "I'll give up chocolate," we'll say, "Don't give it up, just limit it to some on the weekend."

The key is to practice self-leadership by becoming your own personal health manager. You manage your indiscretions in order to promote healthy eating and healthy living. That's what happened to a leader we'll call Joe Higgins, whose life transformed after he adopted a Fit to Lead lifestyle.

The Executive Who Learned to Wait

Joe Higgins looked whipped the first time he walked in the door of the Cooper Clinic. He was fifty-six, an age when he should have been feeling empowered by the fruits of a successful political career and energized by a high-level executive position with an international company.

But for Joe, the burden of his medical problems hung on his six-foot frame like an election gone sour. He had gout, elevated cholesterol, and high blood pressure, a trio of ailments that were tangible proof that his no-diet, no-exercise lifestyle had finally caught up with him.

Joe was a sweets kind of guy: cakes, pies, desserts of all kinds, the creamier the better. That's one of the reasons he had gout, a disease that Ben Franklin suffered from that used to be called "the rich man's disease." And like many high rollers, he was a social drinker who enjoyed his bourbon at the dozens of business and social functions that regularly commanded his attention. What he didn't know was that every drink, every cream puff, was killing him calorie by calorie.

It was the treadmill test that had put him over the edge. After just thirteen minutes of walking with EKG leads taped to his chest, he cried "uncle" and stepped off the moving mat. His Cooper Clinic rating? Joe scored in the "very poor" category, the absolute bottom of the fitness barrel.

Even worse, his stress test was abnormal. His blood pressure was elevated, and his blood pressure response to exercise was not appropriate. In short, Joe was a perfect candidate for a heart problem.

Joe's fitness tests were a wake-up call—a message that he decided to accept and change. He started an exercise program with a simple routine of walking fifteen minutes a day and plunged into the Fit to Lead diet. During the week he completely eliminated desserts, cut back on his alcohol, and stuck to a dietary plan emphasizing low-fat proteins, fruits, and vegetables. On the weekends, he splurged.

"If I want to have a steak, I have a steak," he says. "But I won't have a big sirloin. Instead I'll have a petit filet."

As for exercise, he worked his way up—to three miles of jogging and a ten-minute mile. Within a year, he dropped from 205 pounds to 165, he eliminated his blood pressure medicine, his cholesterol profile had improved, and his gout had completely disappeared.

Perhaps most impressive of all is his current state of fitness. Ten years after his first visit, Joe, who is now in his late sixties, rates "superior" on the treadmill and has even been known occasionally to jog around Houston's Memorial Park with former President George Bush.

For eleven years Joe has been following the Fit to Lead routine, and he's never fallen back. He has gone from being a pudgy middle-aged executive on a downhill health spiral to a dynamo pushing seventy who keeps going like the Energizer Bunny! He's not a guy who runs marathons. He's not a dietary purist following a slavish dietary routine. He's simply a guy who found his diet and exercise rhythm by being "good" during the week and having occasional "bad" splurges on the weekend.

Joe Higgins was a common nondieter who jumped on the Fit to Lead bandwagon and never fell off. But what if you're the opposite of Joe—a chronic dieter and exercise hater who has never succeeded at keeping off the pounds? You can do it, too. The Fit to Lead program works for all.

Why the Fit to Lead Program Will Work for You

There are five good reasons to start on the Fit to Lead program no matter how many times you've yo-yoed back and forth on other programs.

1. **It is realistic.** This program is based on normal eating and exercise for normal people. We've designed it for people like us, who need an approach that is simple and straightforward. The way we see it, if a diet isn't tasty and satisfying, if it requires exercise that we hate, it doesn't work.

2. **It's easy to follow.** You can adapt the Fit to Lead program to your busy lifestyle. We've worked with enough executives to know about the common business trips, frenzied runs around town to fit in errands, and dining at fast-food and regular restaurants. We've specifically designed the program around such a busy lifestyle. The exercise program requires no equipment. You can do it in your office, hotel room, or living room. And the eating plan requires no complicated food preparation or mathematics. In fact, you can continue to eat out. We'll just show you how to make fitter menu choices. You can stay on this program successfully.

3. **It's built around personal rewards.** The Fit to Lead program allows you to reward yourself. In Chapter 5, you'll learn more about self-rewards, as well as seven other important mental tactics that will help keep you on track.

    Executives know this mind-set and can help to apply the same standards to their employees. These rewards can become a motivator. In Tedd Mitchell's family, for example, every Friday night is Mexican night, and his kids are so eager for this that they have even refused sleepovers at a friend's house on Friday evenings!

4. **It's life changing.** By implementing this type of a change in your dietary and exercise habits, the Fit to Lead program reinforces positive behaviors that become a way of life. With time, the craving for some of those foods that had previously left you bloated and mad at yourself in the past tend to decline. The fatigue that once kept you from exercise wanes, and you won't be able to stop yourself from moving. More energy means more productivity!

5. **It's health changing.** Are you suffering from high blood pressure? Backaches? Snoring? High cholesterol? If so, there is probably nothing wrong with you that losing twenty pounds won't fix! That's the advice the Cooper Clinic physicians give to many of their patients—and we pass it on to you. Unfortunately, we've discovered that many people would rather pop a pill than lose weight. By following the Fit to Lead lifestyle, you may actually turn around some of your own medical problems and not only add years to your life but also life to your years!

What the Fit to Lead
Program Is *Not*

As we said before, we won't make lofty promises. You will lose weight (if you need to) and become more productive at work. But this will happen gradually, not overnight.

The Fit to Lead program does not promise

- **magic or miracle foods.** Foods don't burn or melt fat away. Though some foods can certainly help you feel satiated, making you less likely to overeat, there are no "superfoods" that can undo the long-term effects of overeating and lack of activity. If you reduce calories and increase physical activity levels, you'll burn calories from stored fat and lose weight.

- **rapid weight loss.** Sound weight-loss plans promise a gradual weight loss of just one to two pounds per week. Studies show that gradual weight loss increases your success of keeping it off permanently because your body doesn't enter "survival" mode, and your metabolism continues to run at its optimal rate.

- **no exercise.** According to the American Heart Association, "Simple activities like walking or riding a bike are important tools to losing and maintaining weight loss. Yet many 'fad' diets don't emphasize easy changes." An increase in any daily activity that fits your lifestyle will help you burn more calories. Regular exercise also helps bolster your metabolism and lower your appetite. Study after study shows exercise is the true magical key to weight-loss success.

- **all-you-can-eat foods.** Diets that emphasize or disallow certain foods—for example, unlimited amounts of cabbage soup or grapefruit or no dairy or carbohydrate-rich foods—should raise concern. In addition to being unhealthful, cutting out certain foods or entire food groups may increase the likelihood that you will cheat on the diet.

- **fat-melting food combinations.** Eating the "wrong" combination of foods does not cause them to produce toxins or turn to fat. No scientific studies show that combining or sequencing specific foods enhances weight loss.

- **rigid menus.** Limiting food choices and adhering to specific eating times is a daunting, unpleasant task. Instead, look for a plan you can realistically follow for a lifetime—one that emphasizes a variety of grain foods, vegetables, fruits, lean meats, and low-fat dairy products.

- **iron-clad willpower.** Many diet and fitness programs put the onus on you. "If you only tried harder, you would succeed," they tell you. Yet you don't need to try harder to succeed. Willpower doesn't just magically surface out of nowhere! Rather, you must embark on a reasonable exercise and nutritional program custom fit to your unique lifestyle, and you must pair it with psychological exercise through self-leadership to help you achieve success.

Remember: You're in the Driver's Seat

So now you know why and how the Fit to Lead program will work for you. You're almost ready to get started. But before you move on and learn about the exercise plan, we suggest that you make the following two important promises.

1. **I promise not to rush.** We know how tempting it is to want to lose weight and get fit quickly. However, as we've said, lasting results take time. Resist the urge to speed weight loss by skipping meals or holding yourself to a stricter exercise plan than we suggest. Resist the urge to exercise even longer and harder than suggested. Promise yourself that you'll take baby steps toward fitness so that you can maintain lasting results.

THE FIT TO LEAD CREED

What does Fit to Lead mean?

It does NOT mean working out four hours a day in order to run 26.2 miles.

It does NOT mean eating only rice cakes and carrot sticks all day and every day.

It does NOT mean having muscles like Arnold Schwarzenegger.

It DOES mean eating the appropriate foods and mix of food types as outlined in this book.

It DOES mean embarking on an exercise program that focuses on endurance, strength, and flexibility.

It DOES mean practicing the self-leadership strategies necessary to overcome challenges in your journey to becoming more fit.

It DOES mean encouraging others to lead themselves to fitness in their lives.

Most of all, Fit to Lead DOES mean taking control of your diet and exercise behaviors so that you can

- feel energetic and full of passion
- handle the hectic demands of a busy executive
- achieve the goals of your organization and your own personal goals and dreams

2. **I promise to make fitness a priority.** This is the most important promise you can make to ensure success. Schedule your exercise sessions into your day planner with all of your other important appointments. Make yourself and your body your number one priority. And know that once you become Fit to Lead, your improved energy and outlook will make all of your other priorities so much easier to reach.

What's Standing in Your Way?

Before you begin your journey to become Fit to Lead, you must confront some common beliefs that may hold you back from achieving your fittest potential. Here are six common myths about fitness and healthful eating that often serve as roadblocks to success.

Myth #1. Deviation from my plan means I failed. Forget feeling guilty over lapses. We encourage you to have at least one meal each week where you "go for it" and eat whatever you want. Also, taking scheduled breaks from exercise on the weekends is also helpful in keeping the program going. That way you can develop a "workweek" mentality about good eating and exercising. And the program will be more palatable in the long term. Setbacks are part of a successful long-term process. Things happen. Setting your expectations too high and trying to adhere to a schedule that is not realistic only sets you up for failure. Taking a respite from the routine rejuvenates your drive to stick with the plan.

Myth #2. No pain, no gain. Too many executives live their business lives according to this creed. For many, success in business means personal sacrifice, and this extrapolates over to all aspects of their lives. Exercise and dietary programs tend to be on again–off again and intense. Keep in mind that you are far better off following a moderate routine of exercise and dietary discretion than you are knocking yourself out infrequently or sporadically. Most benefits derived from exercise and diet are obtained through consistent but more moderate efforts. A no pain, no gain mentality not only is unnecessary but also counterproductive to the busy executive.

Myth #3. If I'm not overweight, I don't need to exercise. Wrong! The health benefits of exercise are well established for a number of illnesses, and obesity is only one of them. Just because you are lean, don't assume that you are healthy. High cholesterol, high blood pressure, diabetes, and heart disease occur in lean people too. In fact, some data suggest that you are better off fat and fit than skinny and sedentary!

Myth #4. Weight training "bulks you up." While it is true that weight training increases muscle tissue density when properly done, it does not lead to bulkier or larger muscles unless the intensity of the program is really cranked up. It's important to remember that at about age forty, people start losing lean body mass (muscle). You can lose as much as 1 percent of your muscle mass per year after forty, which can mean real trouble by the time you are seventy! Daily tasks that you previously took for granted, such as yard work, carrying groceries, or even carrying luggage at an airport, become difficult. A routine of appropriate strength training prevents this downhill slide and substantially improves quality of life.

Myth #5. Exercise has become so high-tech that it can't be done without help. As executives, you've seen what happens when simple ideas are made complicated. Keep in mind that simple things count. For example, what's the best exercise? Well, the answer is the one you will do! As in business, developing a program that is easy to implement, easy to maintain, and fits into your schedule is the key to success. Leave the high-tech frenzy to others, unless that particular format is suited for your personal style.

Myth #6. As long as I stay fit with exercise, nutrition isn't important. You really are what you eat (and drink). It doesn't make sense to pour crude oil into a high-performance Indy car and expect it to function properly. Likewise, nutrition based on beer, nuts, potato chips, and brewskis doesn't give your engine the fuel it needs for effective performance. Intense, hard-core, extremely restrictive dietary programs are unnecessary and rarely successful. But a sound nutritional program that emphasizes fruits, vegetables, and low-fat proteins has clearly been shown to improve long-term health.

Chapter Three

No More Excuses

We Designed the Fit to Lead Exercise Plan for Executives with Demanding Work and Travel Schedules. It Has Worked for Some of the World's Busiest Executives, and It Will Work for You.

If exercise could be packed into a pill, it would be the single most widely prescribed—and beneficial— medicine in the nation.

—Dr. Robert Butler, former director, National Institute on Aging

Franklin Yancey, co-owner and manager of College Comfort, no longer experiences afternoon slumps. Sherry A. Petta, CEO of Especially Specialties, can now relax more easily in the evening, no matter how demanding her day at the office. And Jory Berkwits, first vice president of Merrill Lynch in Boston, feels more confident and focused on the job than he did thirty years ago.

Though their amazing results may sound like fodder for a product infomercial, these busy executives found startling energy, confidence, stress relief, and weight control in something that can't be sold or bottled. They found it by committing themselves to regular exercise, the first of three important ingredients in the Fit to Lead program. Indeed, exercise may be the most important tool not only for maximizing your performance on the job but also for bolstering your health for years to come.

You probably know this already, or you wouldn't have bought this book. However, you may not know that exercise can create time in your busy schedule, rather than take time away from it.

Perhaps you've tried to start exercising in the past. You may have stuck faithfully to a program, but then your busy schedule caused you to miss a session, then two. Then you stopped exercising altogether. We've heard that story from many of the executives we've counseled and trained.

Our Fit to Lead exercise program helps counteract such excuses. You can perform the exercises anytime, anywhere, including your office, hotel room, or even airport lounge. You need no specialized equipment. You need only a firm commitment.

Our program includes three important components, designed both to maximize your ability to lead as well as maximize your health.[1]

- **Endurance.** You build endurance through aerobic (also called cardiovascular) exercise such as power walking, jogging, and swimming. Aerobic exercise raises your heart and breathing rates. As you'll soon learn, more endurance creates more energy. You'll increase your ability to breathe oxygen and have it delivered to the body cells that need it. This in turn boosts your mental and physical stamina at work.

- **Strength.** You build strength by moving your muscles against resistance. This helps increase both the size and strength of individual muscle fibers, allowing you to lift heavier weights for a longer period of time. Increased strength makes airport travel less strenuous as well as naturally improves your posture, which helps you to look and feel more confident. "By far the biggest benefits I've gained from fitness are self-confidence and self-esteem," says Berkwits. "I'm not talking about how I look in a mirror, but rather how I feel inside. I feel good when I wake up in the morning."

- **Flexibility.** When you stretch your muscles on a routine basis, they become more flexible, allowing you to move more fluidly with a greater range of motion. More flexible muscles also possess a greater ability to build strength and endurance, which helps you boost the first two aspects of fitness. They also help you to withstand the rigors of sitting or standing for long periods of time without back pain and other discomforts.

You Can Do It at Any Age!

Here's the most exciting news about fitness—you can improve your endurance, strength, and flexibility at any age.

But the longer you put fitness off, the more you lose.

Without endurance exercise, for example, your heart's ability to pump efficiently will drop approximately 30 percent between age thirty and seventy, and the rate of decline will increase after age seventy.[2] Yet our extensive research done at the Cooper Aerobics Center of more than 100,000 people reveals that this significant decline in endurance or aerobic capacity does not have to occur for executives over forty. In fact, executives age forty and beyond can maintain an extremely high level of aerobic capacity simply by walking three miles three to five days a week.

Indeed, numerous studies on the aerobic capacities of older people support these observations about endurance. In one study, eight women and four men averaging seventy-one years of age cycled three times a week for twelve weeks at 60 percent of their maximum work capacity. The participants began with two ten-minute sessions and worked up to two twenty-minute sessions after six weeks. On completion of the program, the participants increased their maximum workload (intensity and duration of bicycling exercise) by 16 percent and their maximum oxygen uptake (a measure of aerobic capacity) by 11 percent.

In another study, forty-nine veterans over age sixty-four with chronic illnesses (e.g., arthritis, hypertension, and heart disease) participated in an exercise program for more than four months. The regimen consisted of a warm-up, stationary cycling, stretching, weight training, walking, and a cooldown. The results showed that the participants averaged nearly a three-minute increase in treadmill times (duration of time on exercise) over their performance prior to the exercise program. Also, their resting heart rates decreased by an average of nearly five beats per minute, an indication of improved aerobic fitness.[3]

Similarly, you can make notable strength improvements well into your seventies and eighties. A particularly destructive tendency of aging is the loss of muscle tissue. Without a regular program of strength exercises—or at least consistent involvement in rigorous, muscle-conditioning activities, such as heavy labor—you'll lose muscle mass steadily after age thirty. According to some estimates, most of us lose 3 to 5 percent of our muscle mass every ten years, beginning between ages thirty and forty. Some experts argue that the total loss of muscle mass between ages thirty and seventy may be as high as 30 to 40 percent, or an average of 10 percent every ten years during this period.[4]

The good news is that strength exercises can help reverse this loss of muscle tissue. In fact, research suggests that you are never too old to reverse the loss of muscle tissue. One study in particular showed that even those over ninety years of age can become stronger and increase the size of their muscles with a supervised weight-training program.[5]

EXECUTIVE ENLIGHTENMENT

"Fitness is so important to me that I waited more than two years to move our offices until a space opened in a building that had a fitness facility," says Gordon G. Miller III, president and CEO of G3 Systems, Inc. "I also hired a personal trainer for one hour a day, three days a week, for six months to help me get into a routine. I scheduled my workouts into my calendar and gave them a high priority. Out of seventy-five appointments, I only missed three. I also bought a world-class treadmill for my home, so I could work out in the mornings with my kids and family. Finally, when traveling, I only stay at hotels with fitness facilities that offer twenty-four-hour access."

You Can Do It with Any Schedule!

With the Fit to Lead exercise program, you need no fancy equipment. You can do the program anytime, anywhere. It's the easiest program around to fit into a busy day.

As you'll soon learn, our endurance program focuses on types of exercise, such as walking, that you can enjoy and do from any location. For our strengthening program, your body weight is all you need to shape up.

In short, we've taken the excuses out of exercise. All you have to do to be successful is make the commitment to do it. That's right, commitment may be the most important thing you do to seal your success. Executives tell us that scheduling exercise into their day planners, just like any other important appointment, provided the best insurance for sticking with their program. They also say that exercising in the morning not only helps ensure that they fit in their session but also allows them to reap the benefits for the rest of the day. Here's how one executive put it.

"I get up every morning around four-thirty and spend anywhere from forty-five minutes to an hour running between
four to five miles," says Charles Barnard, senior vice president
of corporate real estate and southwest regional manager of the
Bank of America. "Running very early in the day allows me to
be outside in the fresh air where I can clear my head and focus
on both short- and long-term goal-setting, as well as the tasks
at hand for the day or week ahead. Exercise as well as a good
diet allow me to have more energy and be more focused
throughout the day."

Here are some additional tips for making fitness work.

- **Use your downtime wisely.** We all experience some
  downtime throughout the day. If you pay attention,
  you'll notice ten minutes here and there when you are
  too angry, tired, or uninspired to work. Those ten
  minutes of downtime can be easily turned into
  exercise time. Go for a brisk walk or do your stretching
  or strengthening routine. You'll find that it will help
  you return to work with more energy, focus, and
  creativity.

- **Schedule it in.** This bears repeating. Schedule a half
  hour to an hour *every day* for exercise. Make it
  nonnegotiable.

- **Stock sneakers in all locations.** Keep a pair in your car,
  at the office, at home, and wherever else you may find
  yourself with some spare time. Then you'll always have
  a comfortable pair of shoes for walking.

- **Learn to multitask.** Many executives we've trained and
  interviewed told us that they conducted business during
  their workouts. They jogged or played squash with
  business associates, for example.

Now that you've firmly committed yourself to the Fit to Lead exercise plan, let's take a look at each of the program's three components: endurance, strength, and flexibility.

The Fit to Lead Endurance Prescription

30+ minutes, 3 to 5 days a week

Regular endurance exercise will boost your ability to lead in startling ways.

First, regular endurance exercise is the best mental therapy around. In fact, numerous studies show that regular endurance exercise boosts mood more effectively than prescription drugs. Endurance exercise such as brisk walking, running, and swimming helps to blast away stress, a common ingredient in the lives of every executive we interviewed for this book.

The inability to effectively handle career stress is what makes you feel fatigued at the end of the workday. It dulls your thinking, making you lose interest in work and life. It makes you feel distracted and unable to focus. Endurance exercise works by boosting levels of brain chemicals that make you feel good all over.

Besides reducing stress, endurance exercise improves your body's oxygen and energy delivery system. Your lungs are able to inhale more air, your heart more effectively pushes blood throughout your body, and your body cells more efficiently burn fuel for energy. Result: You feel less fatigued and more energetic all day long.

"By going for a jog every day, I create more energy and less stress," says Franklin Yancey. "On the few days that I've opted to not exercise, I feel the effects later in the day or later in the week."

Finally, endurance exercise tends to help people sleep better. You fall asleep faster and stay asleep longer.

Whether you chose walking, swimming, cycling, or some other form of movement, your chosen form of endurance exercise will serve as the cornerstone of your fitness efforts. Strive to exercise aerobically for a total of thirty minutes three or more days a week, as research shows this is the amount needed to bolster health and endurance.

Indeed, the "public health statement" regarding physical activity produced by the Centers for Disease Control and Prevention and the American College of Sports Medicine reads: "Every U.S. adult should accumulate 30 minutes or more of moderate-intensity physical activity on most, preferably all, days of the week."[6]

This recommendation parallels the guidelines provided by Dr. Steven Blair, director of epidemiology at the Cooper Institute for Aerobics Research, based on his study of approximately 13,400 men and women. In this study, Blair monitored the health outcomes of men and women for four years. Then he asked them to exercise to exhaustion on a treadmill. Based on their treadmill times, he divided them into five fitness categories and then monitored their health for an additional eight years. At the conclusion of the study, the totally sedentary men, who made up the bottom 20 percent fitness category, had a death rate from heart disease, cancer, diabetes, and stroke that was 65 percent higher than the most active men in the top 20 percent category. Blair concluded that thirty minutes of sustained activity, three to four times a week, significantly reduced mortality from all causes.[7]

This study strongly shows that to reduce the risk of premature death, to prolong life, and to enhance functioning, executives should accumulate thirty minutes of moderate exercise per day.

What type of activity should you choose? Whatever type you

like best and can do most easily. For many executives, this is either walking or jogging, both activities that can be fit into a busy day. Berkwits plays squash at a club two blocks from his office. "I can often squeeze in a game during the busiest of workdays," he says. "Many times I will play squash instead of eating lunch out."

Whatever activity you choose, start out gradually. You have plenty of time to get into shape, so don't inflict sore muscles and fatigue on yourself. Such tactics will only work to derail your motivation.

If you've never exercised before, we strongly encourage starting with a simple walking program, such as the one outlined later in this chapter. You can eventually increase your intensity to jogging or running, but don't feel obligated. Walking is an excellent form of exercise, as the Cooper Institute has found time and time again. In one notable study of 102 women, those who walked a twelve-minute mile burned as many calories and achieved the same heart rates as women who *ran* a nine-minute mile. We also found that slower walkers were able to improve indicators of overall health, such as boosting HDL cholesterol, just as much as faster walkers.

No matter what form of aerobic exercise you choose, start all of your sessions with some abdominal work. This will warm up your body as you strengthen your core muscles. Choose from the following three exercises, completing up to fifteen repetitions or until fatigue, whichever comes first.

Abdomen and Trunk

Curl-ups

1. Lie on your back with your knees bent at about forty-five degrees and your feet flat on the floor. Cross your arms over your chest.

2. Exhale as you lift or curl your upper body toward your knees, bringing your head and shoulders off the floor. Keep your head in a neutral position, as if you were cradling an orange between your chin and chest. Hold for one to three seconds and then lower as you inhale. Repeat for up to fifteen repetitions or until fatigue.

Side Reaches

1. Lie on your back with your knees bent at about forty-five degrees and feet flat on the floor. Place your arms on the floor next to your torso with your palms facing down.

2. Exhale as you curl your chin into your chest and bring your torso up no more than forty-five degrees. At the same time, reach your right hand toward your right heel. You will feel the right side of your abdomen working a bit harder than the left. Inhale as you lower to the starting position. Alternate sides for up to fifteen repetitions or until fatigue.

Hip Curls

1. Lie on your back with your hands behind your head. Bend your knees and raise your feet off the floor. Squeeze your knees together.

2. Exhale as you contract your lower abdominal area and curl your hips up about five inches, bringing your knees up and in toward your chest. Inhale as you lower to the starting position. Repeat for up to fifteen repetitions or until fatigue.

Below is an eight-week walking prescription. For each walk, start off at a slow, easy pace for three minutes to allow your muscles to warm up and your heart to adjust to the effort. Then pick up your pace for the prescribed amount of time. At the end of your walk, cool down by walking slowly for five minutes.

EXECUTIVE ENLIGHTENMENT

"Staying fit with a busy schedule is no different than staying fit with an open calendar," says Jory Berkwits. "In life, you get to make choices. And you also get to be accountable for them. One thing I've learned is that if I ever start feeling a little sorry for myself, if I feel I've had some bad luck or gotten a bad break, all I have to do is look in the mirror. Then I realize that I'm looking at my problem! And when I choose to do something about it, I'm looking at the solution too."

Our program starts with a two-mile walk. If you can't complete that distance, start with what you can handle and gradually add half-mile increments to your walk. Once you can walk two miles, start the program on Week 1.

Before starting the program, measure out a two-mile distance in your neighborhood and near your office so you'll know how far you've walked. High school tracks are a great place to walk or jog a prescribed distance, as one lap around the track equals one quarter of a mile. Of course you may find other physical settings to be more pleasant and provide more variety of things to look at. As long as you identify convenient and practical locations that afford you a good safe place to walk a measured distance, you are on the right track.

Your Fit to Lead Strengthening Prescription

7 exercises, 2 days a week

Endurance and strength go hand in hand. If you fail to perform a strengthening routine as you age—even if you participate in

BEGINNER WALKING PROGRAM

Week	Distance (miles)	Time (minutes)	Number of Days
1	2	36	3–5
2	2	35	3–5
3	2	34	3–5
4	2	33	3–5
5	2.5	42	3–5
6	2.5	40	3–5
7	2.5	38	3–5
8	3	47	3–5

endurance exercise—your muscles will continue to weaken. Eventually your muscles will become so weak that you can no longer maintain your endurance exercise program.

In fact, most people older than thirty are already weaker than they were during their teenage years. Less strength results in a reduced ability to function physically. A case in point is an average ninety-year-old woman who must contract her thigh muscles at their maximum capacity just to stand up from a sitting position in a low chair or to get out of a car.

Second, your strength can indirectly extend your life. A 1988 Danish study indicated that gait disturbances and vision impairment were the two objective health measurements most strongly associated with death during a three-year follow-up among patients seventy-five to eighty-five years of age. This suggests that strength exercises may extend your life because they can enhance your ability to walk efficiently. Third, more strength means less pain and discomfort. It is estimated that

80 percent of all lower back pain is the result of poorly conditioned muscles.[8]

Another important facet of strengthening exercises relates to bone loss. Your bones reach their maximum density between ages twenty-five and forty. After age forty, your total bone mass declines at a rate of up to one-half of 1 percent per year. At menopause, women may begin to lose bone density at an even higher rate of 2 to 3 percent per year. Losing bone density can be dangerous because this results in an increased risk of broken bones and the development of osteoporosis, a disease characterized by brittle, porous bones that fracture easily. Approximately one-third of all women and one-sixth of all men suffer a hip fracture by the time they reach seventy. Strength training, however, can serve as a barrier to bone loss. It's been shown that weight-bearing exercises can help you reach the highest possible peak bone mass by age forty and then retard this gradual loss of bone mass. Those who fail to exercise their muscles, can expect to lose more bone mass than those who do.[9]

Finally, your amount of muscle mass determines your metabolism. Each pound of muscle in your body burns roughly fifty calories a day to maintain itself. The less muscle you have, the slower your metabolism, and the less you can eat without gaining weight.

There are numerous types of strengthening programs, from calisthenics to light circuit weight training to aqua aerobics training. However, we have focused on calisthenics that incorporate body weight as the main resistance. You can do these exercises anytime, anywhere. It's the most effective and convenient form of exercise for executives we could possibly design.

Below you'll find exercises to strengthen your upper and lower body. Choose either the modified or standard push-ups, for a total of seven exercises. Start with one set of each exercise, completing them in the order listed. As you gain strength, you can add one to two more sets, for a total of three sets.

"If I treat exercise and fitness as important as returning a phone call to a client or being on time for an appointment, I will fit it in. If I think of it as just something to do in my free time, I won't fit it in, because I *rarely* have free time," says Franklin Yancey. "Treat exercise as one of your important daily tasks, like showing up for work or going on your lunch break. Most people don't forget to do either."

Move from one exercise to the next in the sequence and then start over, repeating the sequence one to two times.

Start each session by warming up with eight to ten minutes of walking or some other form of movement. Perform each exercise for up to fifteen repetitions or until fatigue, whichever comes first. The repetitions should feel tough, but you should not get to the point that you feel like you can't do another one.

Lower Body

Lunges

1. Stand with your feet hip width apart. Place your hands on your hips.

2. Inhale as you take a large step forward with either foot. Keep both knees bent. Lower your hips toward the floor. Stop when your extended thigh is parallel to the floor. Be sure the knee of the extended leg doesn't go forward of your ankle. If it does, you need to take a longer step when you execute the lunge step.

3. Exhale as you rise to the starting position. Repeat for up to fifteen repetitions or until fatigue for each leg. Perform up to three sets.

Calf Raises

1. Stand with your feet hip width apart and your hands on the back of a chair for balance.

2. Exhale as you rise onto the balls of your feet. Lower and repeat for up to fifteen repetitions or until fatigue.

Squats

1. Stand with your feet hip width apart. Place your hands on the back of a chair or the edge of a desk for balance.

2. Inhale as you bend your knees and sit back, as if you were sitting back into an imaginary chair. Keep your body weight as far back as possible without losing your balance. Try to get your thighs to form a parallel line with the floor.

3. Exhale as you press back up to the starting position and repeat for up to fifteen repetitions or until fatigue.

Upper Body

Modified Push-ups (for beginners)

1. Kneel on your hands and knees. Place your hands, fingers pointing forward, on the floor shoulder width apart under your chest. Straighten and lengthen your spine.

2. Inhale as you slowly bend your elbows and lower your torso toward the floor, making sure to keep your back straight. Imagine that you have a yardstick taped to

your spine and you are trying to keep each vertebra in your spine against the stick. Stop when your chin touches the floor.

3. Exhale as you press yourself back to the starting position. Repeat for up to fifteen repetitions or until fatigue.

Standard Push-ups (for intermediate and advanced)

1. Kneel on your hands and knees. Place your hands, fingers pointing forward, on the floor shoulder width apart under your chest. Extend your left leg, placing your body weight onto the ball of your left foot. Then extend your right leg. Straighten your back and firm your abdomen.

2. Inhale as you bend your elbows and lower your chest toward the floor. Stop when your upper arms form a parallel line with the floor and your chin and chest hover just above the floor.

3. Exhale as you push yourself back to the starting position. Repeat for up to fifteen repetitions or until fatigue.

Arm Lifts

1. Sit on the floor with your legs extended. Place your palms on the floor about six inches behind your buttocks, with your fingers pointing away from your body.

2. Lean back slightly and then exhale as you press your hips toward the ceiling, creating a straight vertical line from your head to your toes and balancing on your palms and feet. Hold for one to three seconds.

3. Inhale as you lower your hips to the starting position. Repeat for up to fifteen repetitions or until fatigue.

Desk Pull-ups

1. Sit on the floor and extend your legs under a desk or sturdy table (one you are sure will not tip over or break when bearing your weight). Grasp the edge of the desk with your hands shoulder width apart.

2. Exhale as you slowly pull yourself up, lifting your hips and buttocks off the floor but keeping your feet on the floor. Stop when your chin clears the desk.

3. Inhale as you lower to the starting position and repeat for up to fifteen repetitions or until fatigue.

Seat Dips

1. Sit on the edge of a sturdy chair. Place your palms on the chair next to your buttocks. Press into your palms to lift your buttocks, bringing them off the chair, until your legs form 90-degree angles.

2. Inhale as you bend your arms and lower your buttocks toward the floor. Stop when your upper arms form a parallel line with the floor.

3. Exhale as you press yourself back to the starting position, making sure to use your arms and not your legs to rise. Repeat for up to fifteen repetitions or until fatigue.

Your Fit to Lead Stretching Prescription

10 stretches, 3 days a week

Research suggests that as you age, your tendons (which connect muscles to bones) and ligaments (which connect bones to bones) tighten up. The outcome of this is loss of range of motion around your joints.

Suddenly, bending over feels more strenuous. You strain to reach something on a high shelf. Regular stretching helps to reverse this tightening, allowing you to sit all day without discomfort.

Besides helping to reverse this loss in flexibility, regular stretching helps to bring circulation to your muscles, joints, tendons, and ligaments. This in turn speeds the healing process and protects you from injury. Regular stretching can help soothe away neck, shoulder, and back pain that may distract you from working to your fullest potential.

Finally, stretching is mentally and physically soothing. Use this natural stress buster whenever you need a break from a demanding task. Stretching for five or ten minutes will renew

---

EXECUTIVE ENLIGHTENMENT

"I dedicate part of my relaxation time during the evening to exercise," says Sherry Petta. "Sitting on the couch watching TV after work doesn't make me feel any better the next day, so I incorporate a brisk walk, sit-ups, push-ups, and other exercise into my evenings. There is no better way to improve relaxation after a hectic day than to start with exercise."

your energy, recharge your batteries, and make you ready to accomplish the most difficult tasks.

Many people find that a quick stretching routine provides the antidote to midafternoon fatigue as well as to the general malaise and tightness from long air or car travel. So keep this routine in mind whenever you need a break or a quick pick-me-up.

For optimal benefits, you must stretch all the major parts of the body, addressed by the following ten-minute routine. You can do this routine just before your strength-training sessions or after your endurance exercise sessions. Fit it in at least three times a week.

For each stretching session, keep the following pointers in mind:

- Stretch just slightly beyond your comfort zone, but do not push to the point of pain.

- Move slowly. Don't bounce or jerk.

- Unless otherwise indicated, repeat each stretch three times, holding the last stretch for thirty seconds.

- Breathe, breathe, and breathe. Breathing delivers oxygen into the muscles to help them relax and lengthen. Exhale into the stretch; inhale when you release.

- If one side of your body feels tighter than the other, hold the stretch on the tighter side twice as long.

- If you have an injury or sore spot, heat up the area with a heating pad before stretching it.

Total Body Stretch

1. Stand, extending your arms overhead. Stretch your hands as far overhead as possible, reaching up through your entire body. Hold for five seconds. Relax and repeat three times.

Side Stretch

1. Stand with your feet about three feet apart. Relax your right arm at your side and extend your left arm overhead.

2. Slowly bend to the right. Try not to allow your left shoulder to roll forward. Hold for five seconds and then return to center and repeat with your right arm extended.

3. Repeat three more times on each side, holding each stretch for five seconds.

Arm and Back Stretches

1. Stand or sit with your right arm extended overhead, your right upper arm near your right ear. Bend your right elbow, dropping your right hand behind your head to your upper back between your shoulder blades. Relax your chin to your chest.

2. Grasp your right upper arm just above the elbow with your left hand, gently pulling your right arm toward the left. Hold for thirty seconds.

3. Repeat with the other arm.

_____

1. Stand with your feet hip width apart and your knees slightly bent. Clasp your hands behind your back. As you inhale, raise your shoulders up, back, and then down so that you open your chest. Feel your shoulder blades squeeze together as you reach down through your knuckles.

2. Exhale as you bend forward from the hips. Rest your stomach on your thighs and deepen the stretch by reaching out through your knuckles as you raise your arms as far as possible. Hold for thirty seconds. Inhale

as your reach through your knuckles and rise to the starting position.

Hamstring and Back Stretch

1. Sit on the floor with your left leg extended and your right leg bent. Place your right foot near your left inner thigh, resting your right thigh and knee on the floor.

2. Lengthen your spine and straighten your back as you bend forward from the hips. Extend your hands to your left shin, ankle, or toes, feeling the stretch along the back of your left leg. Hold for thirty seconds. Repeat on the other side.

3. To stretch your back, round your spine, bringing your head even closer to your foot. Hold for thirty seconds. Repeat on the other side.

Thigh Stretch

1. Stand near a wall with your feet hip width apart. With your left hand on the wall for balance, shift your body weight into your left foot as you raise your right foot toward your right buttock. Grasp your right foot with your right hand and pull your foot as close as you can toward your buttocks. Hold for thirty seconds. Switch legs.

Groin Stretch

1. Sit on the floor with the soles of your feet together and your knees open to the sides in a butterfly position. Grasp your ankles, placing your elbows on your inner thighs.

2. Slowly bend forward from your hips and use your elbows to press your thighs down. Hold for thirty seconds.

Lower Back Stretches

1. Lie on your back with your knees bent and feet flat on the floor. Raise your knees in toward your chest, grasping your shins with your hands. Gently use your hands to pull your thighs as close to your chest as possible. Hold for thirty seconds.

   _____

1. Lie on your back with your knees bent and feet flat on the floor. Rest your arms out to your sides with your palms facing up. Raise your knees in toward your chest.

2. Exhale as you lower your knees to the floor to the right and turn your head to look toward the left. Reach through your left fingertips to try to keep your left shoulder blade on the floor during the twist. Hold for thirty seconds. Inhale as you raise your knees back into your chest.

3. Exhale as you repeat on the other side.

Achilles Tendon Stretch

1. Stand three feet away from a wall. Place your right foot two feet in front of your left. Lean forward, placing your palms against the wall.

2. Keep both heels on the floor as you push against the wall and press back through your left calf. Hold for thirty seconds. Switch legs.

Chapter Four

Eating for Fitness

You Can Stick to a Healthy Diet Without Sacrificing Convenience, Restaurant Meals, or Even Your Favorite Foods. The Answer Lies in Making Smarter Choices.

Doctors are always working to preserve our health and cooks to destroy it, but the latter are the more often successful.

—Denis Diderot

Sherry A. Petta dines out every single day, yet she wears the same clothing size she wore in high school. Richard E. Sorensen, dean of Virginia Tech's Pamplin College of Business, manages to eat huge meals at business meetings—yet weighs ten pounds less than he did thirty years ago. Franklin Yancey often spends his time on the road eating at restaurants. Yet his body fat level remains below 10 percent.

How do they pull it off? With careful planning and fit food choices.

Indeed, following a healthy diet need not take hours of planning, shopping, and food preparation. It doesn't require you to avoid restaurants, fast food, or even frozen food and other convenience items. You can still entertain clients, keep up your travel schedule, and indulge in an ice cream sundae every now and then.

We know because we've talked to numerous executives who did just that. Moreover, our Cooper Wellness Program colleagues have helped countless executives make over their diets—without sacrificing the time they put into their careers or spend with their families.

Jerome, an executive at a large multinational company, was one of those executives.

At age fifty-four, Jerome had participated in an exercise program that had progressed from walking two miles a day three days a week, to jogging and walking, and then finally to running four days a week. Jerome also performed a strength and flexibility program three days a week that included stretches for his back and hamstrings, fifty sit-ups, seven to nine chin-ups, and thirty to forty push-ups.

Then downsizing and internal company turmoil made it necessary for Jerome to put in exceptionally long hours. He began skipping exercise sessions.

During a routine physical examination at the Cooper Clinic, his doctor noticed that Jerome seemed generally depressed, and his physical condition had deteriorated noticeably. He was less alert and articulate than he had been just a few months earlier.

His doctor asked about his diet.

"Oh, I've been so busy lately that I grab something quick whenever I'm hungry. I can't even remember when I was home at a decent hour to have a nice balanced meal with my wife."

"What kind of quick things?" the doctor asked.

"Hamburgers, french fries, tacos, things like that."

As it turned out, Jerome had not eaten more than a half dozen well-balanced meals in the past six months, and he almost never ate fruits or vegetables.

His doctor arranged for Jerome to meet with a nutritionist. The nutritionist's analysis of Jerome's eating showed that he was eating too many calories and was not getting the necessary vitamins and minerals. His physician immediately concluded that Jerome's depression and loss of mental functioning were most likely connected in part to the lack of good nutrition. The doctor placed him on a more sound diet regimen, and within only a week or two, Jerome's mood and mental abilities improved. He also found renewed energy and enthusiasm for his exercise program.

As Jerome's story shows, your Fit to Lead eating habits help support your Fit to Lead exercise habits. Proper nutrition will give you the energy, clarity, and mind-set you need to follow through with your exercise program.

Your exercise program serves as the foundation for your new Fit to Lead lifestyle. Yet without proper nutrition, your foundation will never offer firm support.

A mountain of research suggests that you need both exercise *and* proper nutrition to prevent chronic diseases and achieve optimal health. Good nutrition is thus the second crucial component necessary for optimal executive functioning and performance. A proper diet is an absolute prerequisite for building up the endurance and muscle power that will enable you to function and perform at optimal levels. Too often, however, executives tend to scrape by with less than stellar eating habits. It's understandable given the busy lifestyle many executives lead. Fast-food lunches, client dinners at restaurants, and food grabbed on the go at airports and hotels often add up to too many calories and fat and too few nutrients.

The good news is that you can change your diet without dramatically changing your lifestyle. You can continue to eat fast food—if that's your choice. And you can even eat out every single night without gaining weight. The secret, as we've mentioned, lies in making fitter food choices.

Here you will find eight important Fit to Lead eating strategies. Don't feel pressured to adopt all eight strategies at once. Rather, incorporate one into your life at a time, perhaps focusing on one aspect each week, as we suggest in your Total Life Makeover in Chapter 7.

Step 1. Reduce the Bad Fats, Maximize the Good Fats

Possibly one of the most confusing nutritional topics centers on the three-letter-word *fat*. During the low-fat and nonfat craze of the '80s and '90s, we all cut way back on all sources of fat in an attempt to slim down and shape up. Yet, for many, the efforts backfired.

In the late '90s, researchers began unraveling why most Americans continued to gain weight as well as failed to improve their heart health when they switched from high-fat to low-fat diets. Their findings include two important points.

- **Not all fat is bad for your health.** Some types of fat, such as the monounsaturated fats in nuts and olive oil and the omega-3 fatty acids found in fish and flaxseeds, help to boost mood and energy, as well as quell hunger. Numerous studies show, for example, that people who eat regular servings of nuts or olive oil tend to lose weight. Research also shows that these types of fats are good for your heart, and many even help fend off cancer. Finally, emerging research shows that these fats may help fend off muscle damage caused by exercise, as well as soothe pain and prevent injuries. In other words, the fats found in nuts, nut butters, olives and olive oil, avocados, soybeans, and some types of fish help support the Fit to Lead lifestyle.

- **Not all fat is bad for your waistline.** True, every gram of fat contains 9 calories, whereas each gram of the two other macronutrients—carbohydrate and protein—contains only 4. Yet that doesn't necessarily mean that fat is more fattening. When it comes down to the basics, you need to eat fewer calories to lose weight, and simply switching to a lower-fat diet doesn't always translate to fewer calories. For instance, many nonfat versions of cookies and other snack foods contain just as many calories per serving as their full-fat cousins. How could this be? Because manufacturers often add sugar to make up for the loss of flavor from less fat. Also, research shows that most people eat more nonfat snack foods than they would fuller-fat versions, possibly from a flawed belief that these foods are not "fattening."

The take-home message? All fat is not necessarily bad for your waistline. Don't fool yourself into thinking that eliminating fat is the total diet solution. Rather, cutting back on *unhealthy* fats while maximizing *healthy* fats helps you lose weight, reduce cravings, and feel satiated. Eliminate as much unhealthy fat (saturated fats found in animal products and trans fats found in processed and fried foods) as possible. This will help you to better control your blood cholesterol levels and lower your risk of heart disease and stroke. The more saturated fat you consume, the higher your risk of developing negative health outcomes such as elevated cholesterol, colon cancer, and other diseases.[1]

So the next logical question is: What balance of fat (and the types of fat), carbohydrates, and protein should an executive incorporate into his or her diet? We recommend that adults over the age of thirty follow these guidelines:

- No more than 20 to 25 percent of daily calories should come from fat, and most of these fat calories should come from the "good" fats discussed previously.

- About 50 to 70 percent of daily calories should come from complex carbohydrates (such as fruits, vegetables, legumes, and whole-grain products), not from candies, desserts, or simple sugars, which are classified as simple carbohydrates.

- About 10 to 20 percent of calories each day should be from protein sources (such as fish, poultry, and/or lean meats).[2]

To help you achieve those percentages, follow these tips:

Cut back on animal products. Saturated fat, one of two types of fat known to clog your arteries, is found exclusively in animal products such as beef, chicken, and dairy. You can easily cut back on this type of fat without spending lots of time in the kitchen or shunning restaurant, convenience, or fast food. Simply try these fast switches:

- Switch from whole milk to 2 percent, then from 2 to 1 percent, and then from 1 percent to skim. Cutting back on milk fat in baby steps will help you gradually get used to the thinner consistency.

- If you eat red meat, choose sirloin or top round. These are the leanest cuts of red meat. On steaks, remove visible fat and opt for grilling, so that excess fat can drip away. For ground sirloin, skim off the fat as you cook.

- Remove the skin. Most of the fat in chicken and turkey is found in the skin and just underneath. When buying ground poultry, opt for 100 percent skinless breast meat.

- Go cheeseless. When ordering restaurant entrées, ask about sauces and cheeses that may come melted on top of your meal. These often add up to more excess calories and fat grams than you bargain for. Ask for your entrée to come without sauces and cheese, or scrape them off at the table.

Cut back on trans fat. Found primarily in processed and fried foods, this type of fat (also called hydrogenated fat) is the worst type for your health. However, it's hard to completely cut back on processed foods when you live a fast-paced lifestyle, so choose carefully. Read labels and choose products that don't contain "hydrogenated" or "partially hydrogenated" fats. Don't worry. This isn't impossible. For example, Amy's frozen food sells burritos and other tasty foods that contain a wealth of nutrition for a minimum amount of trans fat. Genisoy makes a number of snack foods low in saturated and trans fats.

Eat fish. When eating out, order fish as often as possible. Naturally low in saturated fat, fish is high in appetite-suppressing protein and low in calories. Some types, particularly salmon and others that swim in cold waters, contain high amounts of mood- and energy-boosting omega-3 fatty acids. Fish is also one of the quickest foods to cook at home. Many types can be broiled in the oven in just ten to fifteen minutes.

Switch from margarine to Benecol. You may remember the butter-versus-margarine debates. We now know that neither of these spreads is good for you. Butter contains saturated fat, and margarine contains trans fats. Fortunately, you have a new option. Various manufacturers have produced spreads made from plant sterols. Sold under brand names such as Take Control and Benecol, these spreads have been proved to lower blood cholesterol levels.

Focus on healthy fats. Allow yourself liberal amounts of healthy fats for snacks. Try natural peanut butter that does not contain hydrogenated oils on whole-grain crackers, trail mix, sandwiches made from sliced avocado and soy cheese, and guacamole.

Read the nutritional information on food packages. These charts usually describe the breakdown of calories, amount of calories from fat, and the percentages of fat that are monounsaturated, polyunsaturated, and saturated. Always select products that are relatively low in saturated fat.

Step 2. Eat 20 to 35 Grams of Fiber Daily

This important nutrient found in whole grain foods, beans, fruits, and vegetables will help lower cholesterol, improve intestinal health, and decrease your appetite. Increasing your fiber consumption will also help to naturally decrease your intake of bad fats.

There are two main types of fiber—insoluble and soluble—and each boosts your food fitness in different ways.

Consuming plenty of insoluble fiber (called this because it does not dissolve in water) has been shown to help prevent or treat various health problems, including colon cancer, diverticulitis, constipation, and obesity. Foods high in insoluble fiber include wheat bran and whole-grain cereals, corn, bran, nuts, seeds, and crunchy vegetables like broccoli and carrots.

Soluble fiber has been shown in some studies to help reduce blood cholesterol levels. In particular, oat bran and oatmeal have been linked in various studies to a reduction of cholesterol. As a result, soluble fiber is considered an important food for lowering the risk of atherosclerosis and heart disease. Good sources of soluble fiber include oats, oat bran, oatmeal, apples, citrus fruits, dried legumes, beans, lentils, barley, peas, potatoes, raw cabbage, strawberries, and the fiber supplement Metamucil.

Your Fit to Lead fiber goal: Consume 20 to 35 grams of fiber per day, with about half coming from soluble fiber and half from insoluble fiber.[3]

Here are some quick and easy ways to do just that:

Start on the right foot. Make breakfast a high-fiber meal every day. You can prepare and eat cold and hot breakfast cereal quickly, and both can net you anywhere from 3 to 12 grams of fiber if you choose carefully. Read cereal boxes and experiment with different types. You don't have to force

EXECUTIVE ENLIGHTENMENT

"I've given up Coke and Pepsi and now drink unsweetened tea, water, and occasionally diet soda. That cut almost 1,000 empty calories from my diet every day," says Gordon G. Miller III. "When I eat fast food, I opt for the plain grilled chicken rather than a Whopper and fries, which saves hundreds of more calories. I try to budget for my fat and calories. I typically consume 300 calories at breakfast, 600 at lunch, and 1,000 at dinner. I allow myself to go over at any meal—and sometimes even two meals if it's breakfast and lunch—but I never go over on all three."

yourself to eat a cereal you don't like, as you have many from which to choose. For an extra fiber punch, mix some fruit such as berries into your cereal.

Eat fruit rather than drink the juice. Though orange juice, apple juice, and others contain a wealth of vitamins, they all lack most of the fiber that comes from eating the real thing. Fortunately, whole fruit doesn't take a lot of time to eat, and most types keep well on top of your desk at work.

Snack on nuts. You may have thought that nuts were a "bad" food, but they are not. They contain heart healthy monounsaturated fat as well as 1 to 4 grams of fiber per ounce. They make a great mid-afternoon pick-me-up.

Go whole over processed. When buying anything that comes in a box or a bag, read the label, opting for whole-grain breads, crackers, cereals, and other foods that contain a few grams of fiber per serving over refined grain products that contain none. More and more convenience food and snack manufacturers, including Frito-Lay, are producing high-fiber options.

Just add beans. Beans contain about 7 grams of fiber per serving, making them fiber powerhouses. Keep a can opener and cans of beans in your desk drawer and add them to as many meals as you can. For example, if you buy soup or a salad at your company cafeteria, add some beans. You can also puree any type of bean—particularly black beans and chickpeas— along with some olive oil and garlic to make a tasty and high-fiber sandwich spread to use instead of mayo and other toppings. Or, buy hummus and other premade bean spreads at the grocery store.

Step 3. Consume Between 1,000 and 1,500 Milligrams of Calcium Daily

Despite popular belief, bone mineral loss is a problem for women *and* men. Unfortunately, a growing number of older men are experiencing osteoporosis—the weakening of bones that affects an estimated twenty-four million Americans.

To prevent this disease, you must consume plenty of calcium, a mineral that helps fill in tiny holes in your bones to keep them strong and prevent fractures. Calcium also protects against high blood pressure, cardiovascular disease, and colon cancer. It may also aid in fat burning.[4]

You need between 1,000 and 1,500 milligrams (mg) of calcium a day, the amount in three to five servings of dairy.

Most executives can get their entire dose of calcium through diet. Yet a daily calcium supplement provides extra insurance that you'll meet your requirement. Calcium supplement amounts vary from product to product, so check the bottle to find out the number of milligrams in each calcium tablet. Look for a supplement that contains at least 500 milligrams of calcium.

Be sure to consult your physician before taking *any* supplements.

EXECUTIVE ENLIGHTENMENT

"When I'm home and too busy to cook, my staple food is a healthy type of cereal with skim milk and topped with fresh berries," says Sherry Petta.

Here are some tips for maximizing calcium consumption:

Spread out your intake. Most people consume the bulk of their daily calcium at breakfast, either from the milk in their cereal or from calcium-fortified juice. Because your body can absorb only about 500 milligrams of calcium at once, take your supplement after a lower-calcium meal, such as lunch, dinner, or a snack, to allow your body to slowly absorb calcium all day long.

Make it quick. You'll find calcium in some unusual places. For example, blackstrap molasses contains some, so use it in recipes or on hot cereal. Here are some other fun—and quick and easy—ways to sneak in calcium:

- Spoon nonfat vanilla yogurt on top of a toasted whole-grain frozen waffle for a high-calcium breakfast.

- Snack on Gogurt, a shelf-stable yogurt that you can store in your desk.

- Order a slice of pizza with anchovies for lunch.

- Try a "skinny" (nonfat) or soy latte.

- Mix spinach in with scrambled eggs.

WHERE'S THE CALCIUM?

Food	Serving	Calcium (mg)
Plain and low-fat yogurt	1 cup	415
Ricotta cheese	½ cup	340
Skim and low-fat milk	8 ounces	300–325
Sardines with bones	3 ounces	324
Swiss cheese	1 ounce	270
Canned salmon with bones	3 ounces	180
Spinach	½ cup	122
Tofu	3 ounces	108
Frozen chopped broccoli	½ cup	94

Step 4. Eat Five to Nine Fruits and Vegetables a Day

Fruits and vegetables rank as the healthiest foods on the planet. They are naturally low in calories, fat, and sodium, and high in heart-healing and disease-preventing nutrients called antioxidants. These nutrients get their name from the fact that they reduce or eliminate damage caused by dangerous, out-of-control oxygen molecules.

These molecules, known as free radicals, are critical to the working of the immune system.[5] When they are present in the body in excessive amounts, however, the immune system ceases to operate properly. In fact, studies suggest that there is a significant relationship between free radical damage and coronary artery disease, various forms of cancer, premature aging, early onset of Parkinson's disease, and eye problems such as cataracts.[6]

Executives may be more susceptible to free radical damage than other workers. Growing research indicates that an increase in free radicals can be caused by factors that executives are exposed to every day—stress, cigarette smoke, air pollution (common in big cities and regular commuting thruways), ultraviolet light, and even certain drugs.[7]

While the body produces some natural antioxidants to fight free radicals, you must eat additional antioxidants for optimal protection. Researchers are still unraveling the science of antioxidants, but they suspect the most powerful ones include vitamin C, vitamin E, beta-carotene (the precursor to vitamin A), folic acid, vitamins B_6 and B_{12}, and selenium, among others. These are all found in abundance in fruits and vegetables.

A nutritional program that includes optimal dosages[8] of antioxidants has the potential to

- increase protection from any form of cancer

- strengthen defenses against heart disease

- preserve eyesight via the prevention of cataracts

- delay the onset of aging

- develop a more powerful immune system

- decrease the risk of Parkinson's disease

In addition to providing the needed antioxidants to combat free radicals, many fruits and vegetables are rich in other healing nutrients, such as potassium to combat high blood pressure, calcium to strengthen bones, and folate to prevent birth defects. Finally, fruits and vegetables are naturally high in fiber.

Indeed, a diet high in fruits and vegetables provides the perfect antidote to the frenzied executive lifestyle.

Also, you don't have to spend a lot of time and effort in the kitchen in order to fit more of them into your daily menu.

Here are some tips to help you meet your Fit to Lead Goal of five to nine servings a day:

- **Buy berries at every visit to the grocery store** and use them in everything. Blueberries, blackberries, raspberries, and others contain a wealth of important vitamins and antioxidants, and they are easy to prepare. Simply wash them and sprinkle them on top of any dish, from breakfast cereal to yogurt to ice cream. You can also mix them together and eat them plain as a snack.

- **Keep whole fruit in plain view.** Keep a bowl of apples, oranges, nectarines, peaches, bananas, and other whole fruit on the kitchen table and grab a piece every time you leave the house for work. You can snack on it during a commute or a quick break. Note that while bananas are higher in calories than many other fruits, they are still a good nutritional choice when compared to other snacks (e.g., candy bars).

- **Order extra vegetables when eating out.** Most restaurant entrées come with a serving of starch and a serving of vegetables. Ask for vegetables or salad instead of french fries or rice.

- **Use spinach on everything.** Spinach is packed with nutrition and is easy to include in your diet. Buy a bag of prewashed baby spinach and slip it into sandwiches, sauté it into scrambled eggs, add it to store-bought soups, or simply microwave it in the bag and eat it as a side dish.

Step 5. Eat Smarter Fast Food

From time to time, all of us succumb to the temptation of fast food. It's a given.

Fast-food restaurants cater to the executive lifestyle. In every town you find the same fast-food restaurants as at home. They all deliver food within minutes for just a few dollars.

The problem, as you know, is that most fast food contains way too much fat and too many calories. For example, a Big Mac contains 590 calories and 34 grams of fat (most of it saturated). Along with supersize fries (610 calories, 29 grams of fat) and a small Coke (150 calories), you've consumed more than your entire day's fat allowance and almost your entire day's calorie allowance in one meal!

But this doesn't mean you must dramatically change your lifestyle if fast food has become a way of life. You simply must learn to eat smarter. Here are some tips:

Plan your meals. If you are trying to cut back on fast food, your first step involves meal planning. If you know you have quick-and-easy food at home ready to cook (such as a piece of fish and some broccoli), you'll be less likely to stop off at a burger hut on your way home.

Know the menu and ask plenty of questions. Thanks to the changing tastes and demands of Americans, many fast-food chains now offer healthy and low-fat and calorie options. For example, Subway sells great-tasting subs that all have fewer than 500 calories. McDonald's offers a number of salads low on calories and fat.

Here are some good options:

- Opt for grilled chicken, but ask for the sauce (often packed with saturated fat) to be served on the side. Or scrape it off the bun. Also, many fast-food restaurants coat the bun with oil or butter before grilling. Ask for a plain bun. Then flavor your chicken with mustard.

- If you're in the mood for a burger, go ahead and indulge. Just hold yourself to a plain one—no cheese and no sauce. A McDonald's plain hamburger contains only 280 calories and 10 grams of fat. It's the extra burger, cheese, and sauce of other burgers that pack on the fat and calories. To make your burger even healthier, ask for extra tomato, lettuce, and onion.

- Take advantage of the premade salads and salad bars of many fast-food chains and grocery stores. But avoid the salad fat trap. Common salad toppings such as bacon bits, grated cheese, croutons, and creamy dressings can easily add up to too many calories.

- Ask questions. Many menu items may sound healthy but aren't. For example, one fast-food chain's "garden" burger is fried in oil and topped with mayonnaise. Always ask how the sandwich is cooked (grilled vs. fried) and what type of sauce comes on the bun.

Read the nutrition information. Nearly all fast-food chains now offer nutrition information on the Web for all of their menu choices, and most even post it at the restaurant. So read the fat and calorie information on all of the menu options before you order. You may be surprised by some of the best and worst choices!

Look for the "healthy" fast-food chains. Yes, healthy fast-food chains are beginning to pop up in some cities. Topz in Los Angeles offers lean beef burgers and what they call "air fries," fries that contain half the fat of the typical fast-food version. O'Naturals in Falmouth, Maine, offers an all-organic menu of foods not typically seen at a fast-food restaurant, such as Asian noodles. A chain in Florida called EVOS sells soy burgers and Thai salads.

Step 6. Minimize Refined Foods

Refined foods have become a way of life for Americans as well as for busy executives. They come in boxes, shrink-wrap, bags, and other containers. They're usually shelf stable, tasty, and quick and easy to eat as you multitask by reading reports or even conduct a teleconference.

Yet most types also come with a high calorie and fat wallop, and very little nutrition. For example, a mere ¾-ounce serving of potato chips (about ten chips), contains 100 calories and 7 grams of fat, but next to no fiber or vitamins and minerals. A one-cup serving of macaroni made from refined flour contains almost 200 calories, with little or no fiber or vitamins and minerals.

That said, you *can* eat fit without eliminating convenience foods from your diet. Fortunately, many companies are now responding to consumer demand for healthier convenience foods. However, as with fast food, you must choose carefully. Here are some tips and tricks:

Stock your desk with soup. Whether it comes in a can or dehydrated in a box, store-bought soups offer a wonderful opportunity to sneak in fiber, vegetables, and other fit foods. However, you must choose carefully. Eating New England clam chowder for lunch will net you more saturated fat and calories than you need. Opt for clear broth soups. Many soups also come reduced in sodium, so read labels. Choose those that contain a wealth of beans and veggies too.

Stock your fridge with convenient veggies. One of the best inventions in recent history was the microwave-in-a-bag vegetable. Whether it's spinach or mixed greens, these veggies take seconds to prepare, require only a break room microwave to cook, and taste fantastic. Bring a bag with you to work and keep bags in the fridge at home. Other quick-and-easy veggies include baby carrots, salad greens, and chopped broccoli or cauliflower.

Stock your drawer with dried fruit. Dried fruit keeps well in a desk drawer. It doesn't dirty your fingers if you snack on it while reading reports. And it offers a wealth of fiber and nutrition. Just be careful of the amount you eat, as it can add up to a lot of calories. Hold yourself to one serving, such as five dried pear halves or one cup of dried apples.

Step 7. Learn the Art of Quick-and-Easy Cooking

Getting reacquainted with your kitchen is one of the best ways to ensure that you follow a fit lifestyle. This doesn't require lots of time and effort—that is, unless you want it to.

Some people enjoy cooking; others don't. Some people make time for cooking; others don't. Achieving success lies mainly in knowing what type of person you are. If you want to spend time in the kitchen because you enjoy the process and it helps you reduce stress, that's great. Then subscribe to a healthy cooking magazine such as *Cooking Light* and stock up on healthy cookbooks.

However, if you want to spend as little time in the kitchen as possible, here are some tips for creating fast, healthy meals:

Invest in a personal chef. Once considered an extravagance, personal chefs have become much more common

---

EXECUTIVE ENLIGHTENMENT

"I try to balance a large meal at a business meeting with a few smaller meals throughout the rest of the day. This especially helps if I eat a smaller meal before a big business meeting because I'm less likely to overeat at the meeting," says Richard Sorensen.

and much less costly. Consider having one come in once a week to cook up a week's worth of healthy meals. Store them all in the fridge or freezer and eat one or more of these meals a day. Some chefs also offer cooking classes. You can invite a bunch of other executives or colleagues over for the class and accomplish two tasks at once. Here are some Web sites to explore: Diamond Organics (www.diamondorganics.com); Somerset Organics (www.somersetorganics.co.uk/erol/erol.html); Working Dinners (www.workingdinners.com); Healthy-Eating.Com (www.healthy-eating.com).

Order meals by mail. Diamond Organics and other companies now ship healthy meals to your door. Some of these "meal kits" come already prepared and need only a quick zap in the microwave. Others come with all of the ingredients you need along with a recipe for quick and easy assembly.

Make frozen food healthy. Numerous companies, such as Amy's, now sell healthy and tasty frozen food. You can make just about any frozen dish into a healthy meal simply by adding veggies from a freezer bag and beans from a can.

Keep this formula in mind. Too often people shy away from cooking because they feel as if it takes too much time and effort. However, if your only expectation is to eat a healthy source of protein and a fruit or vegetable (or two), then the task seems much less daunting. Here are some quick-and-easy meals that fit that description:

- Grilled or sautéed boneless chicken breast (bought already skinned, deboned, and sliced) along with steamed broccoli

- Pizza made with store-bought crust, canned tomato sauce, light (part-skim) cheese, veggie pepperoni, and spinach (from a bag)

- Broiled salmon with steamed asparagus

- Pasta made with whole-grain noodles, tomato sauce, and frozen veggie "meatballs"

- Pan-fried Cajun catfish (bought preseasoned from the fish counter) along with mixed frozen vegetables. To pan-fry catfish, spray the pan with olive oil and cook the fish on medium heat about three minutes on each side, until it's opaque all the way through.

Cook on the weekends. If you like to cook but have just one free day of the week, spend it making a week's worth of healthy meals. For example, bake up low-fat veggie lasagna along with vegetarian chili made in the Crock-Pot. Or make a large supply of vegetable soup. You can split these industrial-sized meals into smaller servings and freeze them to eat at your leisure.

Step 8. Master the Art of Eating Out

As an executive, you can't escape the restaurant scene. You visit restaurants when you travel and when you entertain clients. But that doesn't mean that you need to overeat and settle for vitamin-vacant meals that pack on artery-clogging fat.

Your first step is to find a few restaurants close to home and work that offer healthy meals. Then make those your regular spots. For on-the-road eating, do some research on the Internet before getting to your location. Many restaurants now offer their menus online for easy access.

No matter what type of restaurant you find yourself, you can usually make a healthy choice. Here are some examples:

- **Steak house.** Choose the sirloin, which is the steak lowest in saturated fat. Most steaks come four or more

EXECUTIVE ENLIGHTENMENT

"Before hitting the road, I prepare by taking along bottled water, sports drinks, and a few supplement bars. If during travel my only option is fast food, I seek out a place that serves chicken baked or grilled meals," says Franklin Yancey. "When entertaining clients, I look for good restaurants that serve a variety of healthy meals. My basic rule of thumb is simply to avoid grease and not drink sodas when I am on the road or too busy to cook."

times the size of what you should eat, so order a salad (substitute it for the fries) to quench your appetite. Then, when you receive your 20-ouncer, plan to eat only a third of it. That's right, the correct serving for meat is six ounces, the size of two decks of cards. Hold yourself to that amount. To stop yourself from eating— steaks *are* tempting—cut off the third you plan to eat as soon as the steak arrives at the table. Then place your napkin over the two thirds you want to leave behind. You can even ask the waiter to only bring out a third of the steak and to doggie-bag the rest for you to take home for two other meals that week.

- **Japanese.** One word: sushi. You can't go wrong with this high-protein, low-fat meal. Start off with a serving of edamame (soybeans). If you don't know what comes inside a specialty roll, ask. You want to avoid types with melted cheese, mayo, and other high-fat add-ons. If you're eating at a Japanese steak house, order the fish and eat only half as much as they serve you. *Note:* Make sure to tell the waiter to tell the cook to omit any MSG in food preparation.

- **Italian.** Many people opt for pasta at Italian and Mediterranean restaurants, but these places offer a great chance to fit in a fish serving. Order types that come without cheese on top. If ordering pizza, ask them to go light on the cheese.

- **Mexican.** Cheese is the easy downfall here. Get the fajitas and hold yourself to only as many tortillas as come with the meal. Stay away from the sour cream, and you can't go wrong.

WOULD YOU BELIEVE?

Here are the calorie contents of some foods found at popular restaurants:

Cheese fries with ranch dressing	3,010
Fried whole onion with dipping sauce	2,130
Orange beef	1,770
Large movie theater popcorn with butter	1,640
Kung Pao chicken	1,620
Sweet and sour pork	1,610
General Tso's chicken	1,600
The Cheesecake Factory carrot cake	1,560
Fettuccine Alfredo	1,500
House fried rice	1,480

Note: The average person needs about 2,000 to 2,500 calories a day.

Chapter Five

Fit from the Inside Out

Follow Our Eight Steps to Self-Leadership and You'll Easily Confront Obstacles Along Your Journey to Fitness[1]

For most of us, health will depend not on who we are, but on how we live. The body you have at 20 depends on your genes, but the body you have at 40, 60, or 80 is the body you deserve, the body that reflects your behavior.

—Harvey B. Simon, M.D.

We all know how tough it is to motivate ourselves to exercise and eat right. If it were easy to adopt new fitness habits, everyone would do it and succeed. Yet surveys show that between 36 and 43 percent of new exercisers eventually drop out.

Indeed, knowing that fitness can improve job performance and overall health—and knowing how to become fit—is only part of the equation. *Motivating* yourself to get fit is another story. Executives, perhaps, experience the toughest battle when it comes to adopting new fitness habits. Given their jobs, families, and other obligations, they easily can find a long list of reasons to talk themselves out of going for that run or heading to the gym. And it's so much easier to grab fast food than to plan a healthy meal.

So how do the busy executives we interviewed and studied—including President George W. Bush, one of the busiest people in the world—manage to stay fit, to exercise most days of the week, and to watch what they eat? The answer lies in the concept of self-leadership, a motivational system that can dramatically help you achieve all of your personal goals.

First coined by our author team member Chuck Manz, self-leadership can enhance many aspects of your life, including your job satisfaction and fitness habits. We know because we've conducted numerous studies on the topic.

Self-leadership includes both behavioral and mental strategies, the same strategies used by the executives we've studied to achieve their fitness goals.

And you can do the same. To help you successfully lead yourself to fitness and stay on track, we've developed an eight-step process. Tackle each step one at a time, as we suggest in your Total Life Makeover in Chapter 7.

Once you finish the eight-step process, you'll find that your motivation to get and stay fit comes from deep inside. You'll find that your motivation to exercise and eat right is ironclad. Of course, every once in a while, you'll encounter some ex-

EXECUTIVE ENLIGHTENMENT

"A reporter who had looked at my calendar noticed that I had about an hour and a half off per day. I said that is because I exercise every day. The reporter asked if this was an indication that I do not work very hard," says President George W. Bush. "I said, no, it is an indication that I prioritize exercise. . . . I have given some of the greatest speeches of my life while running. . . . Running is therapy, running is a chance to be alone, a chance to think. . . . Running is an opportunity to be outdoors in fresh air. Running is a wholesome and important experience for me."

cuses. But on the whole, the following eight steps to self-leadership will help you to lead your mind and body to fitness much more easily.

Step 1. Observe and Evaluate Yourself

> *"This is the third time this week that I blew my diet while dining at a restaurant. Why do I always overeat when I eat away from my house?"*

The cement that lays the foundation for our self-leadership includes the information we possess about ourselves—in other words, our self-awareness. By observing our own behavior and its causes (for example, why we behave in desirable or undesirable ways), we can uncover clues that will help us understand what we do and why.

Self-observation and -evaluation involves determining when, why, and under what conditions you use certain behaviors. For example, if you feel you are not accomplishing enough each day (e.g., getting your workouts done) because of wasted time, you can study the distractions you experience. Are you spending too much time on trivial tasks or engaged in informal and unproductive conversations? By observing the amount of informal talking you participate in and the conditions that exist at the time, you can learn more about this behavior.

If you spend five hours chatting during the eight-hour workday, you probably have a problem. Furthermore, if most of these conversations begin during a visit to the company watercooler, you have useful information to help you cut down on that behavior.

Here's another example. If you find it difficult to stick to an optimal Fit to Lead diet, self-observation may reveal that you primarily eat inappropriately when at restaurants. If so, it may be that limiting the number of times you dine out can help you avoid temptation.

You can add power to this strategy by writing down your observations. Keep a pen and index cards, a laptop, or a PDA handy to jot down brief notes that you can examine in detail later. Pretend you are a detective who is conducting surveillance—on yourself. You are both the detective and the suspect, and you are trying to reveal as much about your suspect behaviors as possible.

To get started, identify the fitness-related behaviors you feel are especially important that you would either like to increase or reduce in yourself. Perhaps you want to eat less when eating out or get up earlier each morning to fit in a run. Pick one behavior that you would like to begin to work on. Then follow these tips:

- **Keep a record about the behavior** in your PDA, on an index card, or along the margins in your day planner or desk calendar. You can also photocopy the chart on page [75] and use it to record your notes. Make these notes soon after you notice your behavior.

- **Include the date and time** each behavior occurs.

- **Include the conditions** that exist when the behavior is displayed. For example, if you'd like to eat less when eating out, jot down the circumstances of each overeating episode, including your dining companions, choice of restaurant, conversation topics, menu choices, and so on. Where were you standing or sitting? What were you doing just before the behavior occurred? How were you feeling?

    Similarly, if you'd like to get up earlier in the morning, write down the circumstances surrounding each time you sleep in. What thoughts ran through your mind? How late did you stay up the night before?

- **Note any insights** as to why you think the behavior happened.

An important part of this self-observation exercise is to become more aware of *when* you are engaging in the behavior you want to change. As you recognize when the behavior occurs, it will be easier to stop and take time to write down your thoughts about its occurrence. Try to keep the process simple so that you will not be discouraged from using it.

After you have observed yourself and your use of this behavior over time, evaluate your progress. You will be better prepared to take action by setting specific goals to help change the behavior and its effect on your fitness.

BEFORE YOU MOVE ON

Before attempting Step 2 in your journey to more effective self-leadership, we suggest that you intentionally observe yourself. Make notes about a behavior that you want to monitor by using the form below. Make these notes soon after the behavior happens.

Behavior I want to observe this week:

_____

_____

_____

Date	Time	What was happening?	Why do I think it happened?

At the end of the week, answer this question: Was I successful in gaining a better understanding of this behavior? If not, can you think of another way to help yourself keep track of the behavior you want to change? Give it a try! Once you solve one behavior, move on to another one.

Step 2. Set Goals

"Someday I'm going to lose weight.
I'll begin a fitness program one day."

Harvey Mackay once said, "If you don't have a destination, you'll never get there." That brings us to the self-leadership strategy of setting goals, an effective strategy that will help you lead yourself to perform challenging behaviors such as exercising and eating right.

President George W. Bush sets personal goals for his fitness. For example, he set a goal of running a marathon and he achieved this goal. Such longer-term goals help him create the context for setting shorter-term goals to maintain fitness every day. "Running is a chance to set a momentary goal, a daily goal and achievement," he told us.

It is futile to exert effort with no direction. Imagine that you and some friends decide to take a road trip together. Your friends pile into a large van and you climb into the driver's seat. You start the van and head toward the nearest freeway. For a while, everyone is happy and smiling. Then about an hour later someone remarks, "Where are we going?" You reply, "I don't know." Others just shrug their shoulders. After a few minutes, bickering erupts among the passengers because someone wants to go to the beach and someone else wants to go to the mountains. Amid the noise and chaos, you think to yourself, "Wow, this mess could have been easily avoided if we had reached a mutually agreed upon destination before we left."

The same thing can happen to you in your daily activities if you fail to set a destination. In other words, your destination is your personal goal. Every day you "travel" somewhere to a fitness destination. Your traveling involves working toward becoming more fit or less fit. The question that arises is, Do you know what you are working *toward*? Do you know your fitness destination or are you traveling without a clear picture of where you are actually going—without specifically knowing what you are trying to achieve?

Consider the definition of the word "goal," which is "the *result* toward which effort is directed." What is the fitness-related result in which your effort is directed? What are your fitness goals?

Personal goals will help you to direct your self-leadership efforts. But you must set clear, specific, and achievable goals. If you don't have specific goals, you never get anywhere.

Too often people fail because they set unclear goals. For example, you may want to achieve a position of importance and influence in life, but neglect to determine how to go about obtaining the position, or even what the position will be.

Successful self-leaders don't travel without a specific goal. Take some time to think about what you want to accomplish in terms of your fitness level. Here are some tips to help you to set effective goals that will fuel your motivation and lead you to success.

Conduct a self-examination. Before you can establish specific goals, you need to decide what's important to you and what you'd like to accomplish. You need to want to accomplish your self-set goals, so you must truly value your final destination. The goal-setting exercise that follows can help you with this. You've already identified obstacles to your success by completing the self-observation exercise on page 75. Look over your results from that exercise and list a few goals that you think might help you overcome those obstacles.

Avoid fuzzy goals. If you say to yourself, "I want to get in good shape someday," you might have a goal, but you probably won't reach it. One problem is the word "someday." It's unclear and nonspecific. *When* are you going to be in shape? Another problem is that you have not specified *what* "good" means. Also, *how* are you going to do this? The more specific your goals, the more vividly they paint a picture of your destination.

Be realistic. Goals are generally more effective for managing our immediate behavior if they are specific and challenging yet achievable. If we set unreasonable goals that we cannot realistically achieve, we are likely to do more harm than good. Realistic, achievable goals, on the other hand, can be very satisfying when we achieve them. For example, if you have not exercised in years and you set a goal to run a marathon in one month, you are being unrealistic and probably setting yourself up for injury and/or failure. On the other hand, if you want to lose weight and set a goal to lose a pound a week, this is quite realistic and achievable.

EXECUTIVE ENLIGHTENMENT

"I had a roommate who put '3.75' above his computer as a reminder of his goal. He graduated with a 3.5," says Franklin Yancey. "Setting such goals has been a crucial factor for me, both in terms of my exercise habits and my corporate ventures. I wake up every day with a long-term vision in mind and a few shorter-term goals. I tell myself that I can accomplish them no matter how large or important the feat. By setting these goals and creating these visions, I can constantly evaluate where I am and whether I am moving forward to where I want to go."

Set long-term and short-term goals. To achieve success, your goals must address your long-range pursuits as well as your short-run objectives along the way. For example, if you decide on a long-range goal of losing fifty pounds, you need to accomplish many shorter-range goals such as exercising for thirty minutes five days a week.

Another example: If you decide on a long-term goal of being able to run eight miles without stopping, you need to accomplish short-range goals to get there, such as running two miles four times a week. Yet another example includes the long-term goal of writing a book. To do this, you can set a short-term goal of writing five pages a day.

This process takes effort, and although your goals are likely to change over time, it is important that you have current goals for your immediate efforts. Short-term goals help you reach your long-term destination—and if you're reading this book, this destination probably is becoming Fit to Lead.

BEFORE YOU MOVE ON

Before attempting Step 3 in your journey to more effective self-leadership, set a series of short-term goals that will help you achieve your larger goal of fitness. Write those goals here:

Short-term goal 1:
_____

_____

_____

Short-term goal 2:
_____

_____

_____

Short-term goal 3: _____

_____

_____

_____

Step 3. Remove Negative Cues

*"Every time we go to that restaurant, I am overcome
by the dessert display. For the good of my diet,
let's go somewhere else for lunch today?"*

The self-observation exercise you completed in Step 1 taught you what circumstances contribute to certain behaviors. The goal-setting exercise in Step 2 helped you to identify specific short-term steps you can take to help you accomplish your overall goal of becoming Fit to Lead.

Now you're ready to add some firepower to your motivational arsenal. You can take effective steps to change your behaviors simply by eliminating cues that lead to them. For example, if you want to cut down on your consumption of sweets, you can remove the candy dish from the coffee table. Similarly, if you want to spend less time watching television, you can move the TV set to another less frequently used room.

The point is that you are surrounded by physical cues that tend to encourage certain behaviors. If you can identify the things in your world that encourage your undesired behaviors, then you can either remove or alter them. In addition, you can remove yourself from their presence.

For example, if you want to practice the diet principles outlined in Chapter 4, then you might not stock Oreos in your pantry or high-fat ice cream in your freezer. If you want to stop

EXECUTIVE ENLIGHTENMENT

"Exercise is as important, and sometimes more important, as any other activity that I engage in. Therefore, I schedule it into my calendar as I would any other activity," says Richard Sorensen. "If I meet my exercise goals and weight goals, I feel good about myself. I also then feel more comfortable drinking a beer and eating some cheese in the evening, which I enjoy."

snacking late at night, you might spend your time reading a book or magazine rather than watching television, where commercials that depict snacks and food may tempt your taste buds.

Step 4. Increase Positive Cues

"Placing a picture of myself ten years ago on my refrigerator
will really help me stick to my exercise and diet plan.
If I can see the way I look twenty pounds lighter, then this will
motivate me to work out every day and eat right."

Just as you can decrease cues that lead to destructive behaviors, you can also increase cues that lead to desired behaviors. You can do this simply by using physical objects to remind you of, or to focus your attention on, things you want to do.

For example, President Bush relies on this self-leadership strategy when he travels by making sure there is exercise equipment in his hotel room. Having the equipment in his room reminds him of his need to exercise when he travels. Other executives place their treadmill in a room at home that they walk through often, and they place desirable snack foods in plain view to encourage healthful eating choices.

BEFORE YOU MOVE ON

Before tackling Step 5, eliminate some negative cues and develop a few positive cues to help fuel your Fit to Lead exercise and eating habits. Complete the following exercise.

1. How do you use reminders and attention focusers to help you to exercise more and eat better?

_____

_____

2. What are some ways you could improve on your use of reminders and attention focusers?

_____

_____

3. List some negative cues in your life that are discouraging your practice of sound diet and exercise practices.

_____

_____

4. How might you reduce or eliminate these negative cues?

_____

_____

5. List some positive cues in your life that are encouraging your exercise and diet-related behaviors.

_____

_____

6. How might you increase these positive cues?

Step 5. Find Natural Rewards

"This treadmill is so boring. But that rowing machine looks like fun!"

At some point in your Fit to Lead journey, you undergo a critical metamorphosis. Rather than forcing yourself to exercise and eat right, you begin to *enjoy* your new lifestyle. In essence, you become fit from the inside out.

That intrinsic motivation comes from discovering the natural joys and rewards of fitness. Natural rewards cannot be separated from an activity. For example, if you enjoy reading the newspaper and spend a great deal of time doing so, you're engaging in a naturally rewarding activity. You need no incentives to encourage yourself to read the paper. You do it because you enjoy it.

During our interviews, George W. Bush pointed out that the fitness activities he has chosen are ones that he likes to do and that he is pretty good at doing. He doesn't force himself to run. He thoroughly enjoys it.

It seems intuitive that you'll be able to stick only with a new habit that you enjoy. However, too many people fall victim to the false belief that fitness equals displeasure. They assume, perhaps from poorly conducted physical education classes in elementary school or from the no pain, no gain mentality of the '70s, that exercise and boredom, pain, discomfort, and fatigue must all go hand in hand. The belief couldn't be farther from the truth.

In fact, those who most successfully motivate themselves to adopt new fitness and eating habits generally do so by focusing on the joy of movement and newfound health.

To discover the natural rewards of fitness, follow these tips.

Focus on what makes you feel most competent. Simply put, you will enjoy a task that you perform well. For example, a runner in good physical condition may feel strong and powerful, which in turn contributes to feelings of competence.

This doesn't mean that you should start out without a challenge. Small challenges will work to build confidence when you accomplish them. It does mean, however, that you should opt for activities that you feel you can eventually perform well.

Focus on what makes you feel in control. We all have a natural human tendency to want to control our own destinies. For example, most of us prefer to make the decisions that directly affect us, such as where we live and work, whom we marry, and so on, rather than have someone else dictate these decisions to us. In the same way, projects, hobbies, and other activities that we choose to undertake and how we choose to do them contribute to feelings of self-control.

For example, if you pick an exercise activity (e.g., aerobics class) as opposed to letting someone else pick it for you (e.g., the trainer at the gym selects the treadmill for you), your feelings of control of your fitness will be enhanced.

Focus on what gives you purpose. To motivate yourself to exercise daily, you have to decide if it's really important to you, and you need to have a motivating reason for doing it. If it is important to you, then you need to make exercise a priority in your life. For example, if you decide to exercise because your doctor has told you to, you might experience a tough time sticking with your program. However, if you know that fitness will give you more energy to enjoy your life and be a better parent or spouse, you'll probably have an easier time sticking with it.

Very often a deep sense of purpose can be derived from knowing that you are helping others in some meaningful way. And since being fit and healthy enables you to work better and be more effective in general, you may find that a sense of purpose is now built in and you can also be of greater service to others in your workplace, your family, and in other aspects of your life. Conversely, you may discover, as many do, that sticking to a regime—training for a marathon or other fitness undertaking—is easier if done in conjunction with a good cause, like raising money for a specific charity.

BEFORE YOU MOVE ON

Before tackling the next step in this program, take some time to uncover some of your potential natural rewards of fitness and healthful eating. Complete this exercise.

1. List as many activities as you can think of that you naturally enjoy doing, whether they include walking the dog, playing tag with your children, or dancing to salsa music.

---

2. Classify the activities you listed, examining whether they provide you with a sense of competence, self-control, or purpose.

---

3. Identify activities that accomplish all three.

_____

_____

4. Build more natural rewards into activities. Identify pleasant places to exercise or to eat that would increase the natural rewards, or identify things that you can build into the task to make it more naturally rewarding, making you feel more competent, etc. (such as cooking with a loved one).

_____

_____

_____

Focus on the positive, natural rewards rather than the unpleasant parts of fitness. For example, you may choose to run or walk in order to build increased endurance and strength, lose weight, lower stress, and so on. However, you could build in even more natural rewards by running along an ocean shore while listening to the peaceful rhythm of powerful waves. You may run on a forest trail while listening to the singing of birds and the rushing of streams. You simply add rewards by choosing a pleasant setting for your task.

You can also increase feelings of competence by adding a challenge, such as training for a race or charity event. Or you may simply try to tackle more challenging terrain. And you can enjoy more of a sense of purpose if you feel you are setting a positive example for your company or your children.

Step 6. Use Mental Imagery

"Last night before bed, I pictured myself getting up early to go exercise. And you know what, this morning I had the best workout I can recall in a long time. Was this a coincidence?"

John Milton wrote, "The mind is its own place, and in itself can make a heaven of hell, a hell of heaven." What do these words have to do with fitness? A lot, as it turns out.

Your mind plays a huge role in determining what you experience and consequently the world in which you live. Likewise, your mind can affect whether or not you achieve your goals—including your fitness goals. In short, if you think you can become fit, you can. And if you think you are too old, too busy, or too tired to maintain a fitness program, then you are!

To focus your mind on the positive and away from the negative, you can borrow a technique used successfully by athletes for years to enhance their performance. The technique, called mental imagery, involves imagining successful completion of an event before you physically perform it. For example, consider a basketball player who, before a game, pictures himself making all of his free throws. Since he has performed successfully in his mind, he will feel more confident in the "real" game situation and thus have a better chance of making his free throws. And he has programmed his mind for success by mentally practicing the various parts of making a successful shot.

Let's take a look at another example involving you and a colleague at work. Assume that both of you have read the material in this book and have agreed to begin a Fit to Lead program. You picture yourself becoming very frustrated with your workout program because you keep finding excuses to not exercise and eat correctly. You see yourself quitting your fitness program and feeling humiliated as a result. This imagined experience can lead to lack of confidence and poor performance when you actually begin your Fit to Lead program.

On the other hand, your colleague imagines a positive experience (losing weight, feeling more energized) resulting in enormous praise from coworkers and clients. And he pictures just how he is going to accomplish this through a combination of jogging, strength training, and a stretching regimen. Your colleague will likely possess a higher level of self-confidence before starting the actual fitness program, begin to program the necessary behaviors into his thinking, and probably actually enjoy this imagined success.

Your mind is a powerful tool. An exercise that follows will help you find out how powerfully mental imagery can improve your abilities to achieve success. As you attempt the exercise, keep these pointers in mind:

- Visualize your actions, including the important performance details, in normal motion as opposed to slow motion. See yourself performing your actions in real time.

- It may be helpful to mentally picture a "calming" scene such as a beach, a mountain, a forest, a pond, etc., to help you relax before attempting mental imagery.

- Repetition of mental practice is critical. Make sure you repeat the mental imagery steps over and over so that you improve your ability to use mental imagery.

- Space your practice sessions over a number of days, rather than mentally practicing an event in one "mass" session.

BEFORE YOU MOVE ON

Just as a hammer can benefit you only if you know how to use it, mental imagery works only if you know how to use it.

Here are concrete steps to help you use this technique to achieve your fitness objectives. Practice these steps over and over, and you too can enjoy the benefits of mental imagery.

1. Sit in a comfortable chair in a quiet place where you won't be interrupted. Close your eyes.

2. Relax, concentrate, and focus your mind inward. Feel all the stress leaving your body. Beginning at your feet, feel all the stress leaving. Move the stress up your legs, to your chest, then out the top of your head. Let it go, feel it leave. Concentrate all of your energy on this mental practice exercise. Rid your mind of all distractions.

3. Once you feel relaxed and have slowed your mind, focus on a specific challenging situation in which you would like mental imagery to help you perform well (e.g., ordering a healthy menu item when dining out).

4. Talk positively to yourself. Tell yourself several times that you are confident and that you have the power to perform well in this situation.

5. Mentally picture yourself beginning this task, event, or project. Try to maintain your concentration, staying relaxed and focused.

6. Mentally rehearse a successful performance of this challenging situation several times. Picture the details of how you actually do this. It is important that you see yourself in your mind as "an active participant" and not a passive observer. In other words, if you imagine shooting a basketball during a

game, make sure you are standing on the court shooting rather than watching yourself from the stands.

7. Open your eyes. Smile. Praise yourself. You were successful in your mind. Now you should have a greater feeling of confidence that you will perform this event successfully in "real life."

Step 7. Listen to Your Self-Talk

" 'I think I can—I think I can—I think I can—I think I can.' . . .
'I thought I could. I thought I could. I thought I could.' "
—The Little Engine That Could

As children, many of us heard these words spoken by the Little Blue Engine. These same words can benefit you as you strive to attain a more fit you.

This is an example of a mental strategy known as self-talk, that is, the words you mentally say to yourself. The way the Little Blue Engine talked to itself helped its performance in getting over the mountain. In the same way, self-talk can help you stick to your diet- and exercise-related goals. In fact, if you are currently having problems getting to the gym, eating the right types of foods within a Fit to Lead regimen, it could be related to what you are saying to yourself.

For example, think for a moment. Have you ever told yourself any of the following?

- "I don't have the talent."

- "I don't feel like working out today."

- "I hate to exercise."

- "I don't have enough time to go running today."

- "I've eaten two cookies, so I might as well eat the whole bag."

- "Running on a treadmill is boring."

- "If I don't order dessert like everyone else, I'm going to look like a wimp."

These are examples of what we call "sappers," types of self-talk that sap your energy, your self-confidence, and your happiness. Sappers are destructive; they prevent you from achieving your fitness goals and feeling good about yourself. They do this because what you tell yourself every day usually ends up coming true. If you tell yourself you won't have a good day, you won't. If you tell yourself you can't lose weight, you won't. If you tell yourself that you don't enjoy working out, you won't. It is that simple.

As psychologist P. E. Butler writes:

We all talk to ourselves. What we say determines the direction and quality of our lives. Our self-talk can make the difference between happiness and despair, between self-confidence and self-doubt. Altering your self-talk may be the most important undertaking you will ever begin.[2]

The life of Olympic decathlon gold medal winner Dan O'Brien serves as a real-world example of Butler's words. In 1992, O'Brien failed to qualify for the U.S. Olympic team, despite being a favorite to win the gold medal. In the 1996 Olympic Games, he returned to win the gold medal that had eluded him four years earlier. So what was the difference for O'Brien between 1992 and 1996? Why did he fail in 1992 and then crush the field in the decathlon events in 1996? Quite simply, O'Brien altered his self-talk. As O'Brien remarked:

Now I know what to do when I feel panic, when I'm nervous and get sick to my stomach. . . . Instead of telling myself I'm tired and worn out, I say things like, "My body is preparing for battle. This is how I'm supposed to feel."[3]

For Dan O'Brien, changing his self-talk pushed him to Olympic glory. In the same way, changing your self-talk can influence your journey to become more fit and healthy.

The two exercises below will help you to do just that. Do these exercises in order. The first part asks that you remember past events and what you told yourself at that time. Write your responses below each event. Each question will require a significant amount of thought. Complete Part 1 before you move on to Part 2.

Part 1. Uncover Your Negative Self-Talk

1. What did you tell yourself when you were beginning or thinking of beginning a new diet- or exercise-related program?

   _____

   _____

2. Think of a time that you were feeling very out of shape and depressed.

   _____

   _____

3. Think of a day when you were very busy (perhaps away traveling) and you did not eat in a very healthy manner.

   _____

   _____

4. Think of a day when you were planning on exercising but somehow found excuses not to exercise.

_____

_____

5. Think of a day when you were experiencing some physical symptoms such as a headache or achy muscles.

_____

_____

Take a close look at your responses. Do your self-talk examples contain a lot of destructive sappers, or is your self-talk very supportive and motivating? If the former is true, this is a signal to you that what you are telling yourself may be causing many of the setbacks to your fitness program. In other words, you are the person responsible for "sapping" yourself and stifling your path to becoming more fit.

Part 2. Deal with Negative Self-Talk

Once you realize that you are talking to yourself in a negative way, you can change your self-talk. In the second part of this exercise, identify some of the negative messages that you were telling yourself. Then, next to each example of negative self-talk, write a substitute self-statement that you could have told yourself if you wanted your self-talk to be positive rather than "sapping." The following are two examples to help you.

_____

_____

Negative Self-Talk	Positive Self-Talk
1. I hate running on a treadmill; it is boring.	1. While running on a treadmill may not be as fun as running along a beach, I can make it more fun by listening to music while I run or even watching TV. In fact, I could even use this time to "think," because this is one time in the day when I don't have to answer the phone or e-mail.
2. I'll never lose that extra weight.	2. I will lose this weight. It will take a lot of determination and willpower, but I can do it. I will achieve my goal of losing one pound a week.

Now examine your negative and alternative positive self-talk. Do you see a pattern? Do you see that the negative self-talk can be demotivating and that it seems to sap your progress toward exercising more and eating better? On the other hand, do you notice that the positive self-talk is motivating and very supportive? Wouldn't you rather give yourself a fitness advantage by making your self-talk positive in the future? Of course you would! Now that you are aware that your self-talk may be negative and self-defeating and you've practiced changing it to be more positive and constructive, you are well on your way to facilitating the activity you need for becoming more fit and thus becoming a better leader.

Finally, you need to make positive self-talk a habit. Try to be aware of what you are telling yourself over the next several weeks. From the moment you get up in the morning until you go to sleep at night, remind yourself to talk constructively/pos-

Pay attention to your thoughts for the next week. When you catch yourself thinking negatively about exercise and healthy eating, try to replace those thoughts with more supportive/positive ones.

itively to yourself. Repeat this exercise daily until you start to notice that you are having difficulty identifying any remaining negative self-talk and that you have chased all the fitness "sappers" away.

Step 8. Challenge Your Beliefs

*"I've eaten half a bag of french fries.
I might as well eat all of them."*

One of the greatest weight lifters of all time is the Russian Olympian Vasily Alexeev. At one point in his career, he was trying to break a weight-lifting record of 500 pounds. He had lifted 499 pounds but couldn't for the life of him lift 500 pounds, and no other weight lifter could either. Finally, his trainers put 501.5 pounds on his bar and rigged it so it looked like 499 pounds. Guess what happened? He lifted it easily. In fact, once he achieved this feat, other weight lifters went on to break his record. Why? Because they now knew it was possible to lift 500 pounds. Alexeev created a new mental outlook for weight lifters. Once people believed it was possible to lift 500 pounds, they overcame a major barrier to its accomplishment.

The idea that what we believe is possible can be achieved is not new. The amazing fulfillment of many predictions made in books written years ago that attempted to describe the future, such as *Future Shock, Brave New World,* and *1984,* suggests that what we believe can happen *can* happen.

Life problems tend to stem from dysfunctional thinking. Mental distortions form the basis for ineffective thinking that can hinder personal effectiveness and even lead to forms of depression. These distorted thoughts are based on some common dysfunctional beliefs that are activated by potentially troubling or disturbing situations. Based on the work of psychologist David Burns, we specify eleven primary categories of dysfunctional thinking.[4]

1. "Extreme thinking." This is seeing things as black or white. For example, an extreme thinker who finishes a marathon but not within his or her goal time feels like a complete failure.

2. "Overgeneralization." Someone who overgeneralizes tends to see one specific failure or negative result as an endless pattern. For example, if you "cheat" on your diet by eating one Hershey Kiss and berate yourself by saying, "I always cheat on my diet," you're overgeneralizing.

3. "Mental filter." This type of distorted thinking takes a single negative detail and uses it to emphasize and distort all other aspects of one's perception of reality. For example, after several weeks of working out, you receive many positive comments about your appearance, but someone says to you, "Looks like you've put on a few pounds." You obsess about this comment for days and ignore all the other positive comments others have made to you.

4. "Disqualifying the positive." Do you tend to disqualify positive facts from having any relevance or importance? For example, if a coworker tells you that you

look as if you've lost weight, and you respond by thinking, "It must be this outfit. I know I'm as flabby as ever," then you tend to disqualify the positive.

5. "Mind reading." A mind reader draws negative conclusions regarding situations despite a lack of concrete evidence to support these conclusions. For example, if a coworker cancels an engagement to work out with you, a "mind reader" might think, "This person does not think I'm fit enough to keep up with him." But in reality, the coworker canceled because he was not feeling well that day.

6. "Fortune-telling." A fortune-teller arbitrarily predicts that things will turn out badly. For example, a fortune-teller beginning a fitness program might say, "I know this isn't going to work. Nothing has ever worked for me before."

7. "Magnifying and minimizing." This means tending to exaggerate the importance of negative factors and minimize the importance of positive factors related to one's situation. For example, if you are a good dancer but you don't perform very well on a treadmill, you could think, "Why should I bother joining a gym since I'm not very good at running on treadmills and I don't enjoy it either?"

8. "Emotional reasoning." Someone with this type of distorted thinking interprets reality based on the negative emotions he or she experiences. For example, emotional reasoning might lead you to believe, "I feel guilty about not working out today. I must be a rotten person."

9. "Should statements." Statements in one's self-talk that include "should" and "shouldn't" and "ought" and

"must" are used to coerce or manipulate oneself into taking actions. For example, after failing to complete a very difficult aerobic workout, an executive tells herself, "I shouldn't have stopped; I had only fifteen more minutes to go on the StairMaster." This makes her feel so disgusted that she does not exercise for several days.

10. "Labeling and mislabeling." This involves describing oneself, others, or an event with negative labels. The statements "I'm a failure" and "He is a cheat" are examples of mislabeling.

11. "Personalization." This is identifying or blaming yourself as the cause of negative events or outcomes that you are not primarily responsible for causing, or it involves blaming others or your circumstances for your problems. For example, an executive could say, "The reason I'm out of shape is that my schedule is so jammed it does not allow me to eat right or find the time to exercise."

Burns argues that individuals need to confront these dysfunctional types of thinking and replace them with more rational thoughts (beliefs). For example, imagine an executive who attempts to eat in a more healthful manner but ends up actually gaining weight after two weeks on his new nutritional program (due to too much late-night snacking). The executive thinks to himself, "I am a failure. I'll never be able to get fit."

This is an example of dysfunctional thinking based on the distorted belief of "extreme thinking," an individual's tendency to evaluate his or her personal situation in extreme black-or-white categories. The executive is not thinking that some of the most fit managers have failed in some early attempts to start a fitness program. He is obviously evaluating his personal qualities in extremes.

To alter this destructive belief, the executive can identify the dysfunctional thoughts and then replace them with more rational ones. The thought of being a complete failure could be revised to help shift the underlying belief. "Some of the most healthy and fit people have failed in attempts to lose weight and exercise more. I'll learn from this mistake. It's not the end of the world; I will do better next time."

To help overcome such distorted types of thinking, complete the exercise below.

BEFORE YOU MOVE ON

Congratulations for completing the first seven steps to self-leadership. You're almost there. You have just one more exercise to go to complete the final step.

1. Think of a recent time when you were feeling a negative emotion(s) (e.g., stress, anxiety, depression) about your fitness activities. List the negative emotion(s) you were experiencing.

_____   _____

_____

2. What was the fitness-related problem or task that you were facing at the time (e.g., failing to exercise regularly or overeating at a meal)?

_____

3. List some of the things that you were telling yourself at this time:

_____

_____

_____

4. Regarding Step 3, try to identify mental distortions (e.g., "extreme thinking") in your self-talk.

_____

_____

_____

5. How could you change (reword) your self-talk in Step 3 to rid your internal speech of any mental distortions?

_____

_____

_____

A FIT TO LEAD SELF-LEADERSHIP MODEL

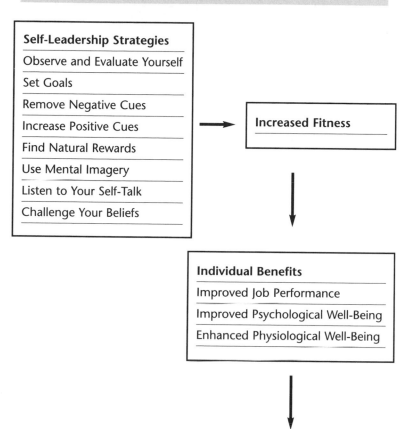

Self-Leadership Strategies

Observe and Evaluate Yourself

Set Goals

Remove Negative Cues

Increase Positive Cues

Find Natural Rewards

Use Mental Imagery

Listen to Your Self-Talk

Challenge Your Beliefs

Increased Fitness

Individual Benefits

Improved Job Performance

Improved Psychological Well-Being

Enhanced Physiological Well-Being

Organizational Success

Part II

Chapter Six

Creating Your
Fit to Lead Plan

Our Seven-Step Process Will Help
Keep You on Track for Years to Come

Most people don't plan to fail, they fail to plan.

—John L. Beckley

Now that you know our three-pronged formula of exercise, nutrition, and self-leadership for developing a *Fit to Lead* lifestyle, your work has just begun. And you're almost ready to start your eight-week Total Life Makeover.

Almost, but not quite.

Before you start exercising, changing your diet, and overhauling your mind, you need to create a Fit to Lead plan. This seven-step plan will help you achieve your goals more easily. You'll complete the first five steps before you start your first exercise session or eat your first healthy meal. These steps will help you to create the framework for success and are outlined in more detail during a "homework" week in the next chapter.

As you learn about each step, consider the story of Connie, a former athlete and current executive who visited the Cooper Clinic recently and used our seven-step process to achieve success on the Fit to Lead program.

Connie was a dean at a prominent university. She had devoted the last twenty years to her family and her work. She was an intelligent, hardworking, get-things-done educator. Furthermore, she enjoyed an exceptional reputation as an excellent administrator. From all appearances, she was quite successful.

When she was young, Connie was active in sports in high school and college. She excelled in school and athletics. Connie was able to maintain an active lifestyle that included her studies and the training necessary to compete at the varsity level.

After graduation, Connie entered graduate school. Like many former collegiate athletes, Connie began to neglect physical activity to focus on her future. She became a professor, married, and began to raise a family. Needless to say, Connie would argue that she just didn't have the time to include fitness in her life. Besides, she would say, "I've put in my time," referring to the athletics of her high school and college days.

By the time she was in her midforties, Connie's lifestyle had changed. The kids were grown. She and her husband were absorbed in their careers. However, for Connie, the demands of her job had become a struggle. She wasn't able to think as clearly as she once did. Her energy level had diminished. She was not sleeping well at night. And she'd noticed that she got out of breath after climbing a flight of stairs.

She realized that unless she made some changes, her chances of continuing her career at a high level were questionable. Recalling her collegiate days, Connie remembered how she managed to maintain her active lifestyle. Connie thought to herself, "Perhaps I should begin to exercise?" That's when the little voice inside of her said, "You don't have the time to exercise." Then she remembered reading the words of author and cardiologist Dr. George Sheehan, that people who say they can't find the time to become fit should realize that an exercise program actually produces time.

That's when she came to us and started her seven-step journey to becoming Fit to Lead.

Step 1. Look in the Mirror

Understand your current situation, what you want,
and forgive yourself for your past.

In analyzing how people change their fitness habits, Dr. Bess Marcus of Brown University developed the Stages of Change model. Her theory is that people can most effectively make changes in their lives if they tackle those changes in small, manageable steps. According to Marcus, your first step to making long-lasting change involves determining "where you are." This will help you find out how ready you are to change your fitness and eating habits.

Let's face it, no one gets out of shape overnight. Twenty extra pounds don't just appear one day. In fact, it usually takes about twenty years of accepting and forgiving ourselves for having that annual two-pound weight gain to eventually creep up to twenty extra pounds. So why don't we just put the process in reverse? In other words, let's accept and forgive ourselves in our current situation. In addition, a realistic assessment of where you are today can become a catalyst for maintaining a Fit to Lead lifestyle. In your Total Life Makeover in the next chapter, you'll learn numerous ways to assess your current situation. For now, let's take a look at how Connie responded.

Connie made an honest assessment of her current fitness level with the help of a fitness professional. She realized that she wasn't going to be able to return to her former collegiate shape. However, she did know that, with time, she could get into excellent shape for her age.

She forgave herself for not staying fit and realized that she couldn't make up for the times she didn't exercise. So, as a way to stick to her new program, she told herself that every time she exercised she was making up for three times she didn't. Obviously, this was a psychological benefit, not a physiological one. However, she knew that this self-talk might help her overcome a common erroneous mental hurdle to starting, or restarting, an exercise program— that is, a feeling that it is useless to begin a fitness program when it's been so long since she exercised and dieted appropriately.

Step 2. Set a Date

Set a date to begin (and notify others of your intentions) your fitness and self-leadership efforts.

By setting a date to begin your fitness and self-leadership efforts, you set in motion the process of shifting the desire to enjoy a Fit to Lead lifestyle into a reality. So commit yourself right now to starting and sticking to the program by picking a date within the next two weeks to start your journey. Try to pick a day that will allow you a little more free time than usual, to eliminate any possible first-day procrastination.

Write your start date here: _____

Now that you've chosen a Fit to Lead start date, it's time to notify others of your intentions. Too often people try to make big changes within a cloak of secrecy. That way, if those changes never materialize, no one knows of your failure to commit to a program. Yet the very act of keeping your goals private sets you up to fail.

Resist the urge to keep your journey secret! Telling others about your efforts will help you harness more power to achieve your goals. That power is teamwork. You've probably heard the well-known proverb that states, "The best potential in 'me' is 'we.'" Indeed, including others in your quest for a Fit to Lead lifestyle automatically creates an accountability/support system. Before moving on to Step 3, tell at least three people about your goals.

Connie decided to begin her exercise program right away. She so-

licited her husband, coworkers, and friends to hold her accountable for an essential ingredient for a successful fitness outcome—showing up.

Step 3. Choose Your Tracking and Scheduling Method

Record and track your progress with a journal, day planner, computer program, or Web site.

By keeping daily records and monitoring fitness progress, you can enhance your ability to stick to the program. These tracking methods help you to notice small rewards and accomplishments along your journey. Pick a tracking method that you feel most comfortable in using. You may prefer a day planner like the one you use in business. Or you may prefer to use a computer program if you have achieved the "cybernirvana" of using a PDA (personal data assistant, aka PalmPilot). Consider plugging into a Web site, such as the one offered by the Cooper Fitness Center (www.cooperfitness.com).

Once you start your program, jot down the following.

- **Every day:** Write down your fitness efforts. How far did you walk or run? Did you perform strength training or stretching?

- **Once a week:** Write down possible measures of success, such as your weight and measurements. Also, on a scale from 1 to 10 (1 being poor and 10 being fantastic), plot your energy level, sleep habits, and mood.

To track her progress, Connie used an exercise log that was available on the Cooper Fitness Center Web site. This worked well for her, since Connie spent quite a bit of time at her desk using a computer.

Step 4. Customize Your Plan

Your ability to stick with new habits involves wrapping those habits tightly around your unique lifestyle, personality, and current health.

In the next chapter, we provide a day-by-day eight-week planner with suggestions for exercise, nutrition, and self-leadership. This program is gradual and designed to take you from flabby to Fit to Lead. That being said, no one program fits every single executive. You may already possess some fitness and therefore find the first few weeks of the program too easy. You may have already mastered a few of the nutrition or self-leadership concepts. For example, if you never eat fast food, you won't need to tackle that step on the nutrition program.

Then again, you may have a health condition that requires you to start out even more slowly than the program we suggest. Or you may know that your personality requires you to make smaller, more gradual changes.

That's where customization comes in. One of the most important things you can do to succeed is firmly plant yourself in the driver's seat of your program design. To succeed, you must commit to improving your fitness, nutrition, and self-leadership habits. However, how quickly you move and where you start and how you accomplish those goals largely depend on you.

We suggest that you start your customization efforts by visiting your doctor for a physical. This is particularly important if you have not been involved in fitness activities up to this point. Find out your blood pressure, cholesterol levels, and other variables. Talk to your doctor about your efforts and explain the program in detail. Ask your doctor his or her opinion.

Then sit down and ponder how you most want to tackle

these changes. We offer additional tips about how to customize our Total Life Makeover in the next chapter. For now, take a look at how Connie did it.

After receiving a physical fitness assessment from her trainer, Connie knew she needed to start out nice and easy. Besides being out of shape, Connie didn't want to "drag a leg" back to work after exercising. Furthermore, due to Connie's busy schedule, her trainer suggested that she begin her program using the "Ten-Minute" method. Connie was to show up at the fitness center and exercise for ten minutes on a piece of cardiovascular equipment (e.g., stationary bike, treadmill, stepper, etc.) for the first two weeks. After the initial two weeks, Connie would add a minute each day until she was up to thirty minutes of cardiovascular (aerobic) exercise. After she had been performing thirty minutes of cardiovascular exercise for two weeks, Connie began to include twenty minutes of weights twice a week. Shortly afterward, Connie began to perform some stretching exercises three times a week for ten minutes. Soon, Connie was able to exercise for an hour five days a week.

Step 5. Get Started!

At the risk of using a worn-out, motivational phrase,
"Just do it!"

You'll complete the next two steps as you progress along your program. But you can't move onto Steps 6 and 7 until you get started! Start your Total Life Makeover today.

After a while, Connie was able to prioritize exercise. The method she utilized was a bit humorous. She realized that if she made an appointment in her Day-Timer, she would keep the appointment. So she decided to put Dr. Cooper's name in the time she designated for exercise. Connie knew she would never put off an appointment with someone like Dr. Cooper.

Step 6. Assess Your Progress

*Once you begin your Total Life Makeover, you'll continually
perform Steps 6 and 7. They will help you stay on track and
remain satisfied with your progress and results.*

During Step 6 you will periodically assess your progress. Look
over your tracking method. How well are you sticking to the
program? Where are you slipping? Check your results. Is your
cholesterol dropping? Are you losing weight, feeling more energetic?

If you notice that you are slipping, ponder what adjustments you must make to improve your success. How are you
doing with your progress? Prioritize your adjustments.

*Connie decided to assess her progress every twelve weeks. She
knew that by doing so, any significant results would emerge. In addition, this short-term time frame permitted Connie to encourage
herself to reach her goal of achieving a Fit to Lead lifestyle.*

Step 7. Adjust Your Program

*Implement needed changes to optimize your
Fit to Lead program.*

Each time you assess your progress, you will probably realize
that you must adjust your program slightly in order to make it
mesh more with your life and habits. Make your adjustments
one at a time. Remember, if it's too fast, it won't last.

*After a couple of months, Connie noticed that the fitness center
where she exercised offered instruction in karate. Her trainer suggested that her balance and self-confidence would be enhanced if
she included karate in her program. So Connie now participates in a
karate class once a week. After a year of exercising, Connie's mental*

sharpness has returned, she has more energy, she is sleeping well, and she has lost most of her excess weight. In addition, she feels at least ten years younger. By all accounts, Connie has become Fit to Lead. Oh, we almost forgot, she's accepted a position at a prestigious university . . . as president.

THE FIT TO LEAD PLAN AT A GLANCE

- **Step 1. Look in the mirror.** Gain an understanding of your current situation and what you want, and forgive yourself for your past.

- **Step 2. Set a date.** Set a date to begin your fitness and self-leadership efforts. Notify others of your intentions.

- **Step 3. Choose your tracking and scheduling method.** Select a method to record and track your progress (e.g., journal, day planner, computer program, or Web site such as the one available through the Cooper Fitness Center).

- **Step 4. Customize your plan.** Identify the fitness components (e.g., cardiovascular endurance, muscular strength and endurance, flexibility, and nutrition) and self-leadership strategies (e.g., to support the process) that will be built into your plan.

- **Step 5. Get started!** Begin your exercise routine and your healthy diet.

- **Step 6. Assess your progress.** Track your progress and compare your results with your fitness objectives.

- **Step 7. Adjust your program.** Make changes as needed to adapt your program to your specific needs and to help you become Fit to Lead.

Chapter Seven

Your Total Life Makeover: The Eight-Week Plan

Your Journey to a Lifetime of Fitness Takes Place One Day at a Time

To be prepared is half the victory.

—Miguel de Cervantes

Now it's time to get started!

This day-by-day fitness makeover will take you from flabby to fit within eight weeks. It incorporates the three elements of the Fit to Lead program—exercise, healthy eating, and self-leadership techniques—each day. However, you'll never feel overwhelmed because you'll take small steps on your journey.

Week 1 starts with some walking at a slow pace. But by Week 8 you'll speed up your pace and lengthen your distance.

The strength-training workout incorporates just three exercises into each session. You can do all of these exercises in your office or hotel room, and you can fit them around your day.

You'll do your stretches after your walking sessions. However, your goal is to stretch three times a week. If another time works better for you, that's fine—as long as you do it!

Before you get started, however, you have some homework. This program kicks off with five planning sessions—based on the first five steps outlined in the previous chapter—to help you develop your Fit to Lead plan. Review the first five steps from Chapter 6. You might be able to complete all five tasks within one session. Or you can space them out over five days.

Your Planning Session

This planning session is very important. Doing these simple steps will build a solid foundation for your fitness program.

Step 1. Assess Your Health and Fitness.

Remember Step 1 from Chapter 6? Have you taken a good look in the mirror? We mean a true, honest look at your abilities?

Probably not. You may sense that you are out of shape. You may sense that your energy is waning and that you're not performing as well as you did ten to fifteen years ago, but we strongly encourage you to get a clear picture of your fitness and health now. This will fuel your motivation to begin, and it will help you to see your results down the road.

Start with a checkup from your doctor. Find out and record the following:

Your weight: _____
Your blood pressure: _____
Your total blood cholesterol: _____
    LDL cholesterol: _____
    HDL cholesterol: _____
    Cholesterol ratio: _____
    Your waist-to-hip ratio: _____

Next, do some personal measurements. On a scale of 1 to 10, with 1 equaling terrible and 10 equaling terrific, rank your level of

Initial energy _____   Post energy _____

Initial stress _____   Post stress _____

Initial control over eating   Post control over eating

habits _____   habits _____

Initial sleep   Post sleep

habits _____   habits _____

You'll rank yourself again in eight weeks.

Then, perform the following tests to assess your current level of endurance, strength, and flexibility.

Endurance

To test your endurance, perform a simple one-mile walking test.

You'll need a stopwatch or digital sports watch and a measured one-mile distance. Four laps around your local high school quarter-mile outdoor track equals one mile. You can also measure a mile in your neighborhood by using your car's odometer.

Walk the entire distance (no running or jogging is allowed). In other words, keep one foot on the ground at all times. Warm up for three to five minutes walking briskly. Then start your stopwatch and walk for one mile as fast as you can without straining. Try to maintain a constant pace for the entire mile. Follow your test with a cooldown, a slow walk for at least five minutes to allow your heart rate and blood pressure to return to normal.

Record your time here in minutes and seconds. Then after eight weeks, do the test again and record your time.

Initial walking time: _____

Postmakeover time: _____

HOW DO YOU MEASURE UP?

To determine your endurance level, refer to the table below. It will help you compare your chronological (current) age to your body age, the age at which your physical and mental capabilities are currently operating. For example, if a fit fifty-year-old man walked the mile in 11:50, his body age endurance would be comparable to someone twenty to twenty-nine years of age.

To determine your body age, look at the table that corresponds to your sex and compare your walking time to your real age. For example, for men, a mile in 11:30 equals a body age of twenty-one. For women, a mile in 12:30 equals a body age of twenty-five.

Men		Women	
Time for One Mile	Body Age	Time for One Mile	Body Age
11:20–12:20	20–29	12:00–12:59	20–29
12:21–13:20	30–39	13:00–13:59	30–39
13:21–14:20	40–49	14:00–14:59	40–49
14:21–15:20	50–59	15:00–15:59	50–59
15:21–16:20	60–69	16:00–16:59	60–69
16:21+	70+	17:00+	70+

Strength

You'll perform a two-part test to assess your strength. For this test you'll need a countdown timer, such as a basic oven or microwave timer.[1]

Part 1: Set your countdown timer to sixty seconds and then perform as many crunches as possible within sixty seconds. Lie on your back with your knees bent. Cross your arms over your chest. Then tighten your abdomen as you crunch up. Make

HOW DO YOU MEASURE UP?

To determine your body age for strength, look at the table that corresponds to your sex and type of sit-up completed and compare your strength-session results to your body age. For example, a man who performs 30–34 sit-ups or a woman who performs 25–29 sit-ups has a body age of between 30 and 39 years.

Men		Women	
Sit-ups	Body Age	Sit-ups	Body Age
40–35	20–29	35–30	20–29
34–30	30–39	29–25	30–39
29–25	40–49	24–20	40–49
24–20	50–59	19–15	50–59

Men		Women	
Sit-ups	Body Age	Sit-ups	Body Age
19–15	60–69	14–10	60–69
fewer than 15	70+	fewer than 10	70+

Men		Women	
Standard Push-ups	Body Age	Standard Push-ups	Body Age
35–30	20–29	45–40	20–29
29–25	30–39	39–35	30–39
24–20	40–49	34–30	40–49
19–15	50–59	29–25	50–59
14–10	60–69	24–15	60–69
fewer than 10	70+	fewer than 15	70+

sure your shoulders and midback (everything from your ribs to your head) rise from the floor for every crunch.

Record the number of crunches you completed here. Then repeat this test in eight weeks.

Preprogram crunch score: _____

Postprogram crunch score: _____

Part 2: Set your countdown timer to sixty seconds and perform as many push-ups as you can within that amount of time. Use proper form, doing them either with your knees on the floor (called a modified push-up) or with your legs extended. (See pages 41 and 42 for proper push-up technique.)

Record the number of push-ups you completed here. Then repeat this test in eight weeks.

Preprogram push-up score: _____

Postprogram push-up score: _____

Flexibility

Finally, to gauge your level of flexibility, you'll do a "sit and reach" test. For this test you will need a yardstick and a foot-long piece of masking tape. Before the test, warm up with gentle stretching or a short walk.

To do the test, place the yardstick on the floor. Then place the masking tape perpendicular to the yardstick at the 15-inch mark. Sit on the floor with your legs extended and feet about one foot apart and the yardstick between your legs. Align your heels with the masking tape, so that the yardstick runs between your legs and your feet reach the 15-inch mark on the stick, with the 0 end of the stick close to your body.

Extend your arms in front of your torso with your fingers touching the floor, placing one hand on top of the other. Exhale as you slowly bend forward from your hips, keeping your back long and straight. Reach your hands forward along the yardstick until you can bend no farther.

HOW DO YOU MEASURE UP?

To determine your body age for flexibility, look at the table that corresponds to your sex and compare your flexibility results to your body age. As a general point of comparison, men who can reach between 17.50 and 17.74 inches and women who can reach between 18.50 and 18.74 inches have a body age of between 30 and 39 years.[2]

Men		Women	
Inches	**Body Age**	**Inches**	**Body Age**
18–17.75	20–29	19–18.75	20–29
17.74–17.50	30–39	18.74–18.50	30–39
17.49–17.25	40–49	18.49–18.25	40–49
17.24–17	50–59	18.24–18	50–59
16.99–16.75	60–69	17.99–17.75	60–69
less than 16.75	70+	less than 17.75	70+

Record the amount of inches your fingers reached on the yardstick here. Then repeat this test in eight weeks.

Preprogram flexibility score: _____ inches
Postprogram flexibility score: _____ inches

Step 2. Set a Date to Start Your Program and Commit to That Date

Record your start date here: _____

Tell three friends of your fitness and eating goals. This will help keep you honest and on track.

Write the names of the three friends here:

1. _____

2. _____

3. _____

Step 3. Pick a Recording Method

This makeover provides space for you to record your results and check off your progress. However, if you're not the type of person who will write in a book, then plan an alternate method. For example, you can record your results in your PDA (such as a PalmPilot) or use a computer program. Or you might jot them down on a wall or desk calendar. Just choose a method that you know you will use.

Step 4. Customize the Program

Read through the following eight-week program and assess how well you think it will fit into your life. Remember, this isn't the only way to get fit. You can custom design your program to your unique needs and schedule.

For example, this plan incorporates walking/jogging, but you should choose a cardiovascular exercise that works best for you. Just do it for the amount of time listed or longer. Also, if you are already exercising aerobically, you might be able to go longer than the suggested amount of time. Or if you are extremely out of shape, you might have to start more slowly. For example, starting with only ten minutes of walking and then adding a minute a week until you can officially "start" the eight-week program.

Now that you've done your homework, it's time for Step 5—getting started! For each day of the next eight weeks, complete the activities that we suggest. Remember: Once you begin using the program and you discover that adjustments are needed for your particular needs, you can still customize the program at any time.

Let's go!

Week 1

During Week 1 of your fitness makeover, you will focus on one nutrition goal and one self-leadership goal.

For nutrition, you will focus on fats. During the next eight weeks, you will keep a food diary, designed to help you see what you eat. You might think that you can do this in your head. However, our experience is that when we just try to remember what we eat, we often selectively forget the unhealthy foods and selectively remember the healthy ones.

Your food diary during Week 1 will help you get a better handle on the types of fats you eat. Write down every type of fat, whether it's the processed trans fats in potato chips or saturated fat in a hamburger. Each day tally up your fat grams, trying to keep them below

- 20–30 grams for women who want to lose weight

- 30–60 grams for women who want to maintain their weight

- 30–60 grams for men who want to lose weight

- 50–75 grams for men who want to maintain their weight

You can do this by making smart substitutions. As you focus on fat, many of these substitutions will come somewhat naturally.

To find the fat grams in common foods that are not labeled, get a calorie and fat gram counter, often sold at the checkout line in grocery stores. You can also go online to the U.S. Department of Agriculture's nutrient database at www.nal.usda.gov/fnic/food-comp.

For self-leadership, you will focus on self-observation. Your food diary will help you to observe what you are eating. But take things a step further. Write down what you notice about your thoughts and actions that contribute or hinder your fitness efforts. When you notice yourself eating too much saturated fat, jot down the circumstances. Were you eating out? Did you plan your meals? Were you feeling stressed? Similarly, if you find that you skip or cut short any of your exercise sessions, jot down the circumstances. Did you stay up late the night before? Did you fail to make it a priority?

Such self-observation will help you to redirect your life in order to more fully support your efforts.

Let's get started.

Day 1

Apply yourself. Get all the education you can, but then, by God, do something.
Don't just stand there. Make it happen.

—Lee Iacocca

Nutritional Fitness

Today I ate: _____ _____

_____

Total grams of saturated fat: _____

Total grams of trans fat: _____

I could have eaten less of these fats by: _____

_____

Body Fitness

Today's stretches: Total body stretch, side stretch, arm and back stretch, hamstring and back stretch, thigh stretch, groin stretch, low back stretch, Achilles tendon stretch

Today's walk: 2 miles within 36 minutes

Mental Fitness

I observed the following thoughts and behaviors today that helped or hindered my ability to stick with my new healthy eating habits and exercise goals (e.g., "When I was eating unhealthy food, not as effective in my exercise,"; "When I was eating healthy food, exercising well").

_____

_____

_____

Day 2

Don't just wish upon a star . . . be one!

—Unknown

Nutritional Fitness

Today I ate: _____

_____

Total grams of saturated fat: _____

Total grams of trans fat: _____

I could have eaten less of these fats by: _____

_____

Body Fitness

Today's strengthening exercises: Modified push-ups, curl-ups, lunges

Mental Fitness

I observed the following thoughts and behaviors today:

_____

_____

_____

Day 3

> *The great dividing line between success and failure can be expressed in five words, "I did not have time."*
>
> —Franklin Field

Nutritional Fitness

Today I ate: _____

_____

Total grams of saturated fat: _____

Total grams of trans fat: _____

I could have eaten less of these fats by: _____

_____

Body Fitness

Today's stretches: Total body stretch, side stretch, arm and back stretch, hamstring and back stretch, thigh stretch, groin stretch, low back stretch, Achilles tendon stretch

Today's walk: 2 miles within 36 minutes

Mental Fitness

I observed the following thoughts and behaviors today:

_____

_____

_____

Day 4

Inaction saps the vigor of the mind.

—Leonardo da Vinci

Nutritional Fitness

Today I ate: _____

_____

Total grams of saturated fat: _____

Total grams of trans fat: _____

I could have eaten less of these fats by: _____

_____

Body Fitness

Today's strengthening exercises: Arm lifts, side reaches, calf raises

Mental Fitness

I observed the following thoughts and behaviors today:

_____

_____

_____

Day 5

There are risks and costs to a program of action. But they are far less than the long-range risks and costs of comfortable inaction.

—John F. Kennedy

Nutritional Fitness

Today I ate: _____

_____

Total grams of saturated fat: _____

Total grams of trans fat: _____

I could have eaten less of these fats by: _____

_____

Body Fitness

Today's stretches: Total body stretch, side stretch, arm and back stretch, hamstring and back stretch, thigh stretch, groin stretch, low back stretch, Achilles tendon stretch

Today's walk: 2 miles within 36 minutes

Mental Fitness

I observed the following thoughts and behaviors today:

_____

_____

_____

Day 6 (optional)

Nutritional Fitness

Today I ate: _____

_____

Total grams of saturated fat: _____

Total grams of trans fat: _____

I could have eaten less of these fats by: _____

_____

Body Fitness

Today's strengthening exercises: Desk pull-ups, hip curls, squats

Mental Fitness

I observed the following thoughts and behaviors today:

_____

_____

_____

Day Off

Yesterday is a cancelled check; tomorrow is a promissory note; today is the only cash you have—so spend it wisely.

—Kay Lyons

One or both days of the weekend are your days off from fitness—your splurge days. Stay focused during the week, but always allow yourself one or two days on the weekend to relax and splurge. Treat yourself to that forbidden food that you crave. Relax on the couch if you want. Congratulate yourself for sticking to the program this week.

Take some time to look over your notes for last week. How did you do? How could you do better? What can you learn from your experiences?

Recommit yourself to success. Tomorrow is a new day. Start it with fitness.

Week 2

Congratulations on your success so far. Let's keep it up!

For Week 2, you will focus on one new eating goal and one new self-leadership goal.

For nutrition, you will work on increasing the amount of fiber you eat each day, aiming to consume 20 to 35 grams. Each day look through your food diary and add up the grams of fiber, studying labels and using a fiber gram counter. Then reflect on how you could make higher fiber choices, such as eating a higher fiber breakfast cereal or whole-grain bread instead of white bread. Try to eat more grams of fiber each day of the week.

For self-leadership, you will focus on setting minigoals. Though your overall goal is to stick to the Fit to Lead program, your journey to fitness will go more smoothly if you set numerous smaller goals along the way. During Week 1, you observed your behaviors, thoughts, and actions. Now you can set goals that will help you change your behaviors. Based on your results from Week 1, set one or more short-term goals for yourself this week, such as going to bed earlier, getting up earlier to exercise, or packing a healthy lunch with fruits and vegetables to bring to work.

Day 1

The key to happiness is having dreams. The key to success is making them come true.

—Unknown

Nutritional Fitness

Today I ate: _____

_____

Total fiber grams: _____

I could have increased my fiber count by: _____

_____

Body Fitness

Today's stretches: Total body stretch, side stretch, arm and back stretch, hamstring and back stretch, thigh stretch, groin stretch, low back stretch, Achilles tendon stretch

Today's walk: 2 miles within 35 minutes

Mental Fitness

How well did you do today to achieve your short-term goals for the week? What could you do to do better?

_____

_____

_____

Day 2

If you wish to soar with eagles, you must be willing to jump off some cliffs.

—Unknown

Nutritional Fitness

Today I ate: _____

_____

Total fiber grams: _____

I could have increased my fiber count by: _____

_____

Body Fitness

Today's strengthening exercises: Modified push-ups, curl-ups, lunges

Mental Fitness

How well did you do today to achieve your short-term goals for the week? What could you do to do better?

_____

_____

_____

Day 3

A journey of a thousand leagues begins with a single step.

—Lao-tzu

Nutritional Fitness

Today I ate: _____

_____

Total fiber grams: _____

I could have increased my fiber count by: _____

_____

Body Fitness

Today's stretches: Total body stretch, side stretch, arm and back stretch, hamstring and back stretch, thigh stretch, groin stretch, low back stretch, Achilles tendon stretch

Today's walk: 2 miles within 35 minutes

Mental Fitness

How well did you do today to achieve your short-term goals for the week? What could you do to do better?

_____

_____

_____

Day 4

A man is what he thinks about all day long.

—Ralph Waldo Emerson

Nutritional Fitness

Today I ate:

_____

_____

Total fiber grams:

I could have increased my fiber count by:

_____

Body Fitness

Today's strengthening exercises: Arm lifts, side reaches, calf raises

Mental Fitness

How well did you do today to achieve your short-term goals for the week? What could you do to do better?

_____

_____

_____

Day 5

It may not be your fault for being down, but it's got to be your fault for not getting up.

—Steve Davis

Nutritional Fitness

Today I ate: _____

_____

Total fiber grams: _____

I could have increased my fiber count by: _____

_____

Body Fitness

Today's stretches: Total body stretch, side stretch, arm and back stretch, hamstring and back stretch, thigh stretch, groin stretch, low back stretch, Achilles tendon stretch

Today's walk: 2 miles within 35 minutes

Mental Fitness

How well did you do today to achieve your short-term goals for the week? What could you do to do better?

_____

_____

_____

Day 6 (optional)

Impossible is a word to be found only in the dictionary of fools.

—Napoleon Bonaparte

Nutritional Fitness

Today I ate: _____

_____

Total fiber grams: _____

I could have increased my fiber count by: _____

_____

Body Fitness

Today's strengthening exercises: Desk pull-ups, hip curls, squats

Mental Fitness

How well did you do today to achieve your short-term goals for the week? What could you do to do better?

_____

_____

_____

Day Off

Saturday and/or Sunday is your day off from fitness—your splurge day(s). Stay focused during the week, but always allow yourself one or two days on the weekend to relax and splurge.

Take some time to look over your notes for last week. How

did you do? How could you do better? What can you learn from your experiences?

Recommit yourself to success. Tomorrow is a new day. Start it with fitness.

Week 3

Congratulations on your success so far. Let's keep it up!

For Week 3, you will focus on one new eating goal and one new self-leadership goal.

For nutrition, you will focus on eating at least three high-calcium foods a day. Pick high-calcium foods that are low in saturated fat (nonfat yogurt is better than regular, skim milk better than whole milk). Each day, record all of the foods you eat in your food diary. Then, at the end of the day, circle the high-calcium choices you made. If you chose fewer than three foods, reflect on how you could make better choices the next day to maximize your calcium intake. Also, if you notice that all of your calcium sources were high in saturated fat, ponder how you might make better choices tomorrow.

For self-leadership, you'll focus on removing negative cues. Reread the section that describes that strategy in Chapter 5 on page 80. Each day this week, take some time to think about what negative cues may be holding you back from achieving optimal success on this program. For example, do you find yourself overeating certain foods? Could you make a choice to not purchase them and thus remove these cues from your home and thereby lower your temptation? Do meals at certain restaurants cause you to overeat? Can you avoid these restaurants? Are you most likely to skip a morning exercise session if you can't immediately find your shoes? Can you place your shoes in a prominent place that you can't miss? Then you can do more brainstorming on ways to eliminate those negative cues.

Day 1

If you think you can, or think you can't, you're probably right.

—Mark Twain

Nutritional Fitness

Today I ate: _____

_____

Circle the high-calcium choices.

How many high-calcium choices did I make? _____

How many of these were high in saturated fat? _____

How can I make better choices tomorrow? _____

Body Fitness

Today's stretches: Total body stretch, side stretch, arm and back stretch, hamstring and back stretch, thigh stretch, groin stretch, low back stretch, Achilles tendon stretch

Today's walk: 2 miles within 34 minutes

Mental Fitness

Examine the foods in your refrigerator, cupboards, and kitchen. Which unhealthy ones do you find yourself eating late at night or in huge amounts? Throw them away.

_____

_____

Day 2

The minute you start talking about what you are going to do if you lose, you have lost.

—George Shultz

Nutritional Fitness

Today I ate: _____

_____

Circle the high-calcium choices.

How many high-calcium choices did I make? _____

How many of these were high in saturated fat? _____

How can I make better choices tomorrow? _____

_____

Body Fitness

Today's strengthening exercises: Modified push-ups, curl-ups, lunges

Mental Fitness

Take a look at your office. What foods do you keep on and in your desk? What unhealthy foods overly tempt you at the cafeteria or vending machine? What steps can you take to avoid these negative cues?

_____

_____

_____

Day 3

If you always do what you've always done, you'll always get what you've always gotten.

—Anonymous

Nutritional Fitness

Today I ate: _____

_____

Circle the high-calcium choices.

How many high-calcium choices did I make? _____

How many of these were high in saturated fat? _____

How can I make better choices tomorrow? _____

Body Fitness

Today's stretches: Total body stretch, side stretch, arm and back stretch, hamstring and back stretch, thigh stretch, groin stretch, low back stretch, Achilles tendon stretch

Today's walk: 2 miles within 34 minutes

Mental Fitness

What negative circumstances prevent you from exercising? How can you avoid these circumstances to better achieve success?

_____

_____

_____

Day 4

Practice does not make perfect; perfect practice makes perfect.

—Vince Lombardi

Nutritional Fitness

Today I ate: _____

_____

Circle the high-calcium choices.

How many high-calcium choices did I make? _____

How many of these were high in saturated fat? _____

How can I make better choices tomorrow? _____

_____

Body Fitness

Today's strengthening exercises: Desk pull-ups, hip curls, squats

Mental Fitness

What people in your life subtly discourage you from exercising and healthy eating? How can you avoid such people, spend less time with them, or enlist them to support your efforts rather than sabotage them, in order to increase your chances of success?

_____

_____

_____

Day 5

To be prepared is half the victory.

—Miguel Cervantes

Nutritional Fitness

Today I ate: _____

_____

Circle the high-calcium choices.

How many high-calcium choices did I make? _____

How many of these were high in saturated fat? _____

How can I make better choices tomorrow? _____

_____

Body Fitness

Today's stretches: Total body stretch, side stretch, arm and back stretch, hamstring and back stretch, thigh stretch, groin stretch, low back stretch, Achilles tendon stretch

Mental Fitness

Notice how sensory cues discourage you from exercising and/or trigger unhealthy eating. For example, watching television exposes you to food commercials, which can trigger late-night snacking. The smell of french fries during your commute home may cause you to pull into a fast-food restaurant rather than waiting until you get home to eat. How can you avoid such sensory cues?

_____

_____

_____

Day 6 (optional)

Hard work won't guarantee you a thing, but without it, you don't stand a chance.

—Patrick Riley

Nutritional Fitness

Today I ate: _____

_____

Circle the high-calcium choices.

How many high-calcium choices did I make? _____

How many of these were high in saturated fat? _____

How can I make better choices tomorrow? _____

_____

Body Fitness

Today's strengthening exercises: seat dips, curl-ups, calf raises

Mental Fitness

Pay attention to any additional negative cues you confront today. What else may subtly discourage you from achieving success? What steps can you take to remove these negative cues?

_____

_____

_____

Day Off

Congratulate yourself for sticking to the program this week. Take some time to look over your notes for last week. How did you do? How could you do better? What can you learn from your experiences?

Recommit yourself to success. Tomorrow is a new day. Start it with fitness.

Week 4

Congratulations on your success so far. Let's keep it up!

For Week 4, you will focus on one new eating goal and one new self-leadership goal.

For nutrition, you will focus on increasing your consumption of fruits and vegetables, aiming to eat at least five to nine servings every day. As you did with high-calcium foods last week, you will now circle all of the fruits and vegetables you list each day in your food diary as well as brainstorm ways to fit in more produce tomorrow.

For self-leadership, you will focus on increasing positive cues to help you stay on track. For example, you might place your sneakers by the door in your office to remind yourself to take a walk, or you might set a bowl of fruit out on the kitchen table to remind yourself to sneak in more produce.

Day 1

There's a difference between interest and commitment. When you're interested in doing something, you do it only when circumstances permit. When you're committed to something, you accept no excuses, only results.

—Art Turock

Nutritional Fitness

Today I ate: _____

_____

Circle the fruits and vegetables eaten today.

How many did I eat? _____

How can I eat more tomorrow? _____

_____

Body Fitness

Today's stretches: Total body stretch, side stretch, arm and back stretch, hamstring and back stretch, thigh stretch, groin stretch, low back stretch, Achilles tendon stretch
Today's walk: 2 miles within 33 minutes

Mental Fitness

Think of a positive cue you can create at home that will encourage you to exercise or eat more healthfully. List that cue here.

_____

Day 2

About the only thing that comes without effort is old age.

—Anonymous

Nutritional Fitness

Today I ate: _____

_____

Circle the fruits and vegetables eaten today.

How many did I eat? _____

How can I eat more tomorrow? _____

_____

Body Fitness

Today's strengthening exercises: Modified or standard push-ups, curl-ups, lunges

Mental Fitness

Think of a positive cue you can create at work that will encourage you to exercise or eat more healthfully. List that cue here.

_____

Day 3

Luck is what happens when preparation meets opportunity.

—Elmer Letterman

Nutritional Fitness

Today I ate: _____

_____

Circle the fruits and vegetables eaten today.

How many did I eat? _____

How can I eat more tomorrow? _____

_____

Body Fitness

Today's stretches: Total body stretch, side stretch, arm and back stretch, hamstring and back stretch, thigh stretch, groin stretch, low back stretch, Achilles tendon stretch

Today's walk: 2 miles within 33 minutes

Mental Fitness

Think of a positive cue you can create at a restaurant that will encourage you to eat more healthfully. List that cue here.

_____

Day 4

It is a funny thing about life; if you refuse to accept anything but the best, you very often get it.

—Somerset Maugham

Nutritional Fitness

Today I ate: _____

_____

Circle the fruits and vegetables eaten today.

How many did I eat? _____

How can I eat more tomorrow? _____

_____

Body Fitness

Today's strengthening exercises: Seat dips, side reaches, squats

Mental Fitness

Think of a positive cue you can use during your commute to work that will encourage you to exercise or eat more healthfully. List that cue here.

_____

Day 5

> *If you find a path with no obstacles, it probably doesn't lead anywhere.*
>
> —Frank A. Clark

Nutritional Fitness

Today I ate: _____

_____

Circle the fruits and vegetables eaten today.

How many did I eat? _____

How can I eat more tomorrow? _____

_____

Body Fitness

Today's stretches: Total body stretch, side stretch, arm and back stretch, hamstring and back stretch, thigh stretch, groin stretch, low back stretch, Achilles tendon stretch

Today's walk: 2 miles within 33 minutes

Mental Fitness

Think of a positive cue you can use in social situations that will encourage you to exercise or eat more healthfully. List that cue here.

_____

Day 6 (optional)

The freedom to fail is vital if you are going to succeed.

—Michael Korda

Nutritional Fitness

Today I ate: _____

_____

Circle the fruits and vegetables eaten today.

How many did I eat? _____

How can I eat more tomorrow? _____

_____

Body Fitness

Today's strengthening exercises: Arm lifts, hip curls, calf raises

Mental Fitness

Think of a positive cue you can use in any area of your life that will encourage you to exercise or eat more healthfully. List that cue here.

_____

Day Off

Take some time to look over your notes for last week. How did you do? How could you do better? What can you learn from your experiences?

Recommit yourself to success. Tomorrow is a new day. Start it with fitness.

Week 5

Congratulations on your success so far. Let's keep it up!

For Week 5, you will focus on one new eating goal and one new self-leadership goal.

For nutrition, you will focus on your fast-food choices. First, pick up a menu along with nutritional information from every fast-food restaurant you tend to visit. Most offer these online. Scour each menu and circle the best choices. Then try to stick to them.

For self-leadership, you'll focus on increasing the natural rewards you reap from exercise and healthful eating. Review the natural rewards exercises in Chapter 5 before getting started this week. Then complete the reflective questions each day.

Day 1

Be like a postage stamp. Stick to something until you get there.

—Josh Billings

Nutritional Fitness

Today I ate:

I made these more fit fast-food choices or didn't eat fast food at all:

Body Fitness

Today's stretches: Total body stretch, side stretch, arm and back stretch, hamstring and back stretch, thigh stretch, groin stretch, low back stretch, Achilles tendon stretch

Today's walk: 2.5 miles within 42 minutes

Mental Fitness

Ponder activities that make you feel competent and in control, and offer a sense of self-purpose. How can you fit more of these fitness activities into your schedule?

_____

_____

Day 2

> Shoot for the moon. Even if you miss it you will land among the stars.
>
> —Les Brown

Nutritional Fitness

Today I ate: _____

_____

I made these more fit fast-food choices or didn't eat fast food at all: _____

_____

_____

Body Fitness

Today's strengthening exercises: Modified or standard push-ups, side reaches, lunges

Mental Fitness

How can you make walking more naturally rewarding? Perhaps simply walking in a different location or with a friend could increase your natural rewards.

_____

_____

Day 3

You never really lose until you quit trying.

—Mike Ditka

Nutritional Fitness

Today I ate: _____

_____

I made these more fit fast-food choices or didn't eat fast food at all: _____

_____

_____

Body Fitness

Today's stretches: Total body stretch, side stretch, arm and back stretch, hamstring and back stretch, thigh stretch, groin stretch, low back stretch, Achilles tendon stretch

Today's walk: 2.5 miles within 42 minutes

Mental Fitness

How can you make your healthful eating habits more naturally rewarding? Perhaps you can involve others you love in your quest, or you might make a game out of it.

_____

_____

Day 4

Great works are performed not by strength,
but by perseverance.

—Samuel Johnson

Nutritional Fitness

Today I ate: _____

_____

I made these more fit fast-food choices or didn't eat fast food at all: _____

_____

_____

Body Fitness

Today's strengthening exercises: Desk pull-ups, curl-ups, squats

Mental Fitness

How can you increase the natural rewards of your strengthening program? Perhaps keeping tabs on the number of push-ups or pull-ups will renew your sense of competence.

_____

_____

Day 5

Big shots are only little shots who keep shooting.

—Christopher Morley

Nutritional Fitness

Today I ate: _____ _____

_____

I made these more fit fast-food choices or didn't eat fast food at all: _____

_____ _____ _____ _____

_____ _____ _____

Body Fitness

Today's stretches: Total body stretch, side stretch, arm and back stretch, hamstring and back stretch, thigh stretch, groin stretch, low back stretch, Achilles tendon stretch

Today's walk: 2.5 miles within 42 minutes

Mental Fitness

How can you increase the natural rewards of your stretching program? For example, doing your stretches just before bed may help you to release any leftover tension and relax you for sleep, creating a treasured bedtime routine.

_____

_____

Day 6 (optional)

One who gains strength by overcoming obstacles possesses the only strength which can overcome adversity.

—Albert Schweitzer

Nutritional Fitness

Today I ate: _____

_____

I made these more fit fast-food choices or didn't eat fast food at all: _____

_____

_____

Body Fitness

Today's strengthening exercises: Arm lifts, hip curls, calf raises

Mental Fitness

List all of the natural rewards you receive from physical, mental, and nutritional fitness. Write them down and place them in a location that you will see often.

Day Off

Take some time to look over your notes for last week. How did you do? How could you do better? What can you learn from your experiences?

Recommit yourself to success. Tomorrow is a new day. Start it with fitness.

Week 6

Congratulations on your success so far. Let's keep it up!

This week you will focus on one new eating goal and one new self-leadership goal.

For nutrition, you will focus on eating fewer empty refined foods and more whole foods. Before you eat a food that comes out of a box, bag, can, or some other container, read the nutrition information. Check out the amount of fat, calories, fiber, and vitamins and minerals in the food. Consider other similar options and look at those labels. Are you making the best choice?

Examine the foods you list in your food diary each evening. Look at labels and do some research to find out if you can find a convenient food to substitute for one that has little to no nutrition.

This week's self-leadership challenge is learning to make the most of mental imagery. Reread the mental imagery section in Chapter 5 on page 87. You will perform the mental imagery exercise on page 89 every night this week before going to sleep.

Day 1

Perseverance is a great element of success. If you only knock long enough and loud enough at the gate, you are sure to wake up somebody.

—Henry Wadsworth Longfellow

Nutritional Fitness

Today I ate: _____

_____

Circle all refined foods.

Other foods with more fiber, vitamins, and minerals that I could substitute for these foods: _____

_____

Body Fitness

Today's stretches: Total body stretch, side stretch, arm and back stretch, hamstring and back stretch, thigh stretch, groin stretch, low back stretch, Achilles tendon stretch

Today's walk: 2.5 miles within 40 minutes

Mental Fitness

Practice mental imagery before bed. Focus on a challenge you encounter at home that may be hindering your fitness schedule.

Day 2

Growing is like running a 26-mile marathon. If we give up on the 24th mile, we will never know what it feels like to finish the race.

—Anonymous

Nutritional Fitness

Today I ate: _____

_____

Circle all refined foods.

Other foods with more fiber, vitamins, and minerals that I could substitute for these foods: _____

_____

Body Fitness

Today's strengthening exercises: Standard push-ups, side reaches, lunges

Mental Fitness

Practice mental imagery before bed. Focus on a challenge at work that may be hindering your fitness schedule.

Day 3

> *Whatever the struggle, continue the climb. It may only be one step to the summit.*
>
> —Diane Westlake

Nutritional Fitness

Today I ate: _____

_____

Circle all refined foods.

Other foods with more fiber, vitamins, and minerals that I could substitute for these foods: _____

_____

Body Fitness

Today's stretches: Total body stretch, side stretch, arm and back stretch, hamstring and back stretch, thigh stretch, groin stretch, low back stretch, Achilles tendon stretch

Today's walk: 2.5 miles within 40 minutes

Mental Fitness

Practice mental imagery before bed. Focus on a social challenge that may be hindering your fitness schedule.

Day 4

Whatever is worth doing is worth doing well.

—Lord Chesterfield

Nutritional Fitness

Today I ate: _____

_____

Circle all refined foods.

Other foods with more fiber, vitamins, and minerals that I could substitute for these foods: _____

_____

Body Fitness

Today's strengthening exercises: Seat dips, side reaches, calf raises

Mental Fitness

Practice mental imagery before bed. Focus on a challenge at home that may be hindering your eating habits.

Day 5

Not everything that is faced can be changed,
but nothing can be changed until it is faced.

—James Baldwin

Nutritional Fitness

Today I ate: _____

_____

Circle all refined foods.

Other foods with more fiber, vitamins, and minerals that I could substitute for these foods: _____

_____

Body Fitness

Today's stretches: Total body stretch, side stretch, arm and back stretch, hamstring and back stretch, thigh stretch, groin stretch, low back stretch, Achilles tendon stretch
Today's walk: 2.5 miles within 40 minutes

Mental Fitness

Practice mental imagery before bed. Focus on a challenge at work that may be hindering your eating habits.

Day 6 (optional)

Our future may be beyond our vision,
but it is not beyond our control.

—Robert Kennedy

Nutritional Fitness

Today I ate: _____

_____

Circle all refined foods.

Other foods with more fiber, vitamins, and minerals that I could substitute for these foods: _____

_____

Body Fitness

Today's strengthening exercises: Arm lifts, hip curls, squats

Mental Fitness

Practice mental imagery before bed. Focus on a challenge you generally encounter at restaurants or social settings that tends to hinder your eating habits.

Day Off

Take some time to look over your notes for last week. How did you do? How could you do better? What can you learn from your experiences?

Recommit yourself to success. Tomorrow is a new day. Start it with fitness.

Week 7

Congratulations on your success so far. Let's keep it up!

This week you will focus on one new eating goal and one new self-leadership goal.

For nutrition, you will focus on increasing your cooking and food preparation skills. Review the food preparation section of Chapter 4. Then each day this week, brainstorm ways that you can improve your cooking and food preparation skills, aiming to try one new tactic each day this week.

For self-leadership, you will focus on your internal self-talk, the thoughts in your head that serve as the spark plugs for your actions—or your lack of action. If you've been experiencing trouble sticking to your program so far, your internal thoughts (what you are saying to yourself) may be to blame. Review the self-talk section of Chapter 5. To get a handle on your self-talk, keep a regular journal throughout the day. You might tote this journal around and jot down thoughts for each day, or you might jot them into your day planner or PDA or desk calendar. Do whatever will help you to remember the internal self-talk you had just before overeating or skipping an exercise session.

Day 1

I am the master of my fate;
I am the captain of my soul.

—William Ernest Henley

Nutritional Fitness

Today I ate:

_____

_____

I tried a new cooking or food preparation skill today.
Yes/No? What was it?

_____

_____

Tomorrow I will improve my food preparation and
cooking skills by:

_____

_____

Body Fitness

Today's stretches: Total body stretch, side stretch, arm and back stretch, hamstring and back stretch, thigh stretch, groin stretch, low back stretch, Achilles tendon stretch

Today's walk: 2.5 miles within 38 minutes

Mental Fitness

List thoughts (self-talk) that led to destructive behaviors today. How can you turn these negative thoughts into positive ones?

_____

_____

_____

Day 2

> *The real voyage of discovery consists not in seeking new landscapes, but in having new eyes.*
>
> —Marcel Proust

Nutritional Fitness

Today I ate: _____

_____

I tried a new cooking or food preparation skill today. Yes/No? What was it? _____

_____

Tomorrow I will improve my food preparation and cooking skills by: _____

_____

Body Fitness

Today's strengthening exercises: Standard push-ups, hip curls, squats

Mental Fitness

List thoughts (self-talk) that led to destructive behaviors today. How can you turn these negative thoughts into positive ones?

_____

_____

_____

Day 3

All that we are is the result of what we have thought.

—Buddha

Nutritional Fitness

Today I ate: _____

_____

I tried a new cooking or food preparation skill today.
Yes/No? What was it? _____

_____

Tomorrow I will improve my food preparation and
cooking skills by: _____

_____

Body Fitness

Today's stretches: Total body stretch, side stretch, arm and back stretch, hamstring and back stretch, thigh stretch, groin stretch, low back stretch, Achilles tendon stretch

Today's walk: 2.5 miles within 38 minutes

Mental Fitness

List thoughts (self-talk) that led to destructive behaviors today. How can you turn these negative thoughts into positive ones?

_____

_____

_____

Day 4

Rule your mind or it will rule you.

—Horace

Nutritional Fitness

Today I ate: _____

_____

I tried a new cooking or food preparation skill today. Yes/No? What was it? _____

_____

Tomorrow I will improve my food preparation and cooking skills by: _____

_____

Body Fitness

Today's strengthening exercises: Desk pull ups, curl-ups, calf raises

Mental Fitness

List thoughts (self-talk) that led to destructive behaviors today. How can you turn these negative thoughts into positive ones?

_____

_____

_____

Day 5

A man is what he thinks about all day long.

—Ralph Waldo Emerson

Nutritional Fitness

Today I ate: _____

_____

I tried a new cooking or food preparation skill today. Yes/No? What was it? _____

_____

Tomorrow I will improve my food preparation and cooking skills by: _____

_____

Body Fitness

Today's stretches: Total body stretch, side stretch, arm and back stretch, hamstring and back stretch, thigh stretch, groin stretch, low back stretch, Achilles tendon stretch

Today's walk: 2.5 miles within 38 minutes

Mental Fitness

List thoughts (self-talk) that led to destructive behaviors today. How can you turn these negative thoughts into positive ones?

_____

_____

_____

Day 6 (optional)

The greatest discovery of my time is that human beings can alter their lives by altering their attitudes.

—William James

Nutritional Fitness

Today I ate: _____

_____

I tried a new cooking or food preparation skill today. Yes/No? What was it? _____

_____

Tomorrow I will improve my food preparation and cooking skills by: _____

_____

Body Fitness

Today's strengthening exercises: Seat dips, side reaches, lunges

Mental Fitness

List thoughts (self-talk) that led to destructive behaviors today. How can you turn these negative thoughts into positive ones?

_____

_____

_____

Day Off

Take some time to look over your notes for last week. How did you do? How could you do better? What can you learn from your experiences?

Recommit yourself to success. Tomorrow is a new day. Start it with fitness.

Week 8

Congratulations on your success so far. Let's keep it up!

For this week, you will focus on one new eating goal and one new self-leadership goal.

For nutrition, you will focus on mastering the art of eating out. To get started, gather up copies of menus at all of the restaurants you typically entertain clients or eat out at with your family. Examine them for healthy choices. If a restaurant offers no healthy choices, don't eat there. If it does, commit yourself to making that food choice before you step in the restaurant's door. Don't even open the menu (unless there are multiple healthy choices for you to choose from). You're having your regular.

This week's self-leadership lesson focuses on developing positive beliefs. Review the material on positive beliefs in Chapter 5. You will practice the positive beliefs exercise each night before bed this week.

Day 1

> *The wisest insights that can be gained by any man or woman is the realization that our world is not so much what it is but what we choose it to be.*
>
> —Charles C. Manz

Nutritional Fitness

Today I ate: _____

_____

Did you eat out? Yes/No?

If yes, did you stick to your smart food choice? Explain why or why not. If you did not, how can you increase your chances of sticking to healthful options in the future?

_____

_____

Body Fitness

Today's stretches: Total body stretch, side stretch, arm and back stretch, hamstring and back stretch, thigh stretch, groin stretch, low back stretch, Achilles tendon stretch

Today's walk: 3 miles within 47 minutes

Mental Fitness

Practice the positive beliefs exercise before bed. Focus on your exercise habits.

Day 2

*One's own thought is one's world. What a person thinks is
what he becomes. That is the eternal mystery!*

—Upanishads

Nutritional Fitness

Today I ate: _____

_____   _____

Did you eat out? Yes/No?

If yes, did you stick to your smart food choice? Explain
why or why not. If you did not, how can you increase
your chances of sticking to healthful options in the future?

_____

_____

Body Fitness

Today's strengthening exercises: Standard push-ups, curl-
ups, lunges

Mental Fitness

Practice the positive beliefs exercise before bed. Focus on
eating out at restaurants.

Day 3

*Aerodynamically, the bumble bee shouldn't be able to fly, but
the bumble bee doesn't know it, so it goes on flying anyway.*

—Mary Kay Ash

Nutritional Fitness

Today I ate:

_____

_____

Did you eat out? Yes/No?

If yes, did you stick to your smart food choice? Explain why or why not. If you did not, how can you increase your chances of sticking to healthful options in the future?

_____

_____

Body Fitness

Today's stretches: Total body stretch, side stretch, arm and back stretch, hamstring and back stretch, thigh stretch, groin stretch, low back stretch, Achilles tendon stretch

Today's walk: 3 miles within 47 minutes

Mental Fitness

Practice the positive beliefs exercise before bed. Focus on developing healthy eating habits at home.

Day 4

> The pessimist sees the difficulty in every opportunity; the optimist, the opportunity in every difficulty.
>
> —L. P. Jacks

Nutritional Fitness

Today I ate:

_____

_____

Did you eat out? Yes/No?

If yes, did you stick to your smart food choice? Explain why or why not. If you did not, how can you increase your chances of sticking to healthful options in the future?

_____

_____

Body Fitness

Today's strengthening exercises: Seat dips, side reaches, squats

Mental Fitness

Practice the positive beliefs exercise before bed. Focus on carving out time for exercise.

Day 5

You see things; and you say, "Why?" But I dream things that never were; and I say, "Why not?"

—George Bernard Shaw

Nutritional Fitness

Today I ate: _____

_____

Did you eat out? Yes/No?

If yes, did you stick to your smart food choice? Explain why or why not. If you did not, how can you increase your chances of sticking to healthful options in the future?

_____

_____

Body Fitness

Today's stretches: Total body stretch, side stretch, arm and back stretch, hamstring and back stretch, thigh stretch, groin stretch, low back stretch, Achilles tendon stretch

Today's walk: 3 miles within 47 minutes

Mental Fitness

Practice the positive beliefs exercise before bed. Focus on self-leadership strategies at work.

Day 6 (optional)

Opportunity is missed by most people because it is dressed in overalls and looks like work.

—Thomas Edison

Nutritional Fitness

Today I ate: _____

_____

Did you eat out? Yes/No?

If yes, did you stick to your smart food choice? Explain why or why not. If you did not, how can you increase your chances of sticking to healthful options in the future?

_____

_____

Body Fitness

Today's strengthening exercises: Arm lifts, hip curls, calf raises

Mental Fitness

Practice the positive beliefs exercise tonight before bed. Focus on any remaining challenges you still face with eating healthy, exercising, and practicing self-leadership.

Day Off

Take some time to look over your notes for last week. How did you do? How could you do better? What can you learn from your experiences?

Recommit yourself to success. Tomorrow is a new day. Start it with fitness.

Fit for Life

Congratulations for successfully completing the first eight weeks of the rest of your life!

By now you should be noticing some of the benefits of your program. Your clothes are probably looser. Coworkers are probably offering compliments about your energy, confidence, and appearance. And you are probably feeling less anxious and more energetic.

At this eight-week juncture, take a day to fuel your motivation even more by assessing your progress. Retake the endurance, strength, and flexibility tests you tried before you started this program and note your progress. Go back to your doctor and find out whether your blood pressure and cholesterol results have improved. Get on the scale or take your measurements. Rate your stress level and sleep habits.

And relish each success!

Then recommit yourself to your new lifestyle. Set new goals. Review your program for what's working and what's not working. Reward yourself and commit yourself to a lifetime of fitness. Great job!

One suggestion for the next step of your fitness journey is to repeat the Body Fitness days of Week 8, while continuing to focus on all the weeks for Mental and Nutritional Fitness. This will allow you to maintain your new fitness levels as you set new goals for the future.

As we close, we'd like you to ponder once again the words written by the late exercise enthusiast, author, and cardiologist, Dr. George Sheehan:

People who say they can't find the time to become fit should realize that a fitness program actually produces time.

Indeed, if you place a priority on fitness and follow our Fit to Lead prescriptions, you will reap more time; you will not only live longer but also gain maximum effectiveness and efficiency. Who benefits? You and the organization that depends on your leadership.

Chapter Eight

Becoming a SuperLeader

Leading Others to Lead Themselves
to Better Health and Fitness[1]

If you're a boss, you should be aware that you can save your company a lot of money and greatly increase the productivity of those under you just by promoting fitness among your workers.

—Kenneth H. Cooper

After implementing the Fit to Lead program into their lives, many executives begin to see their companies and employees differently. Personally, they know that fitness works. They feel more energetic, accomplish more during the day, and can pinpoint concrete results the program has brought them on the job.

Yet they also can't help but notice the lack of fitness in others around them. They notice who looks fit and who does not. They notice how this affects job performance. They want to spread the Fit to Lead philosophy throughout the company.

They wonder whether they are effective leaders, and whether those they lead are effective in their work and life. Perhaps you've come to this same crossroads. Is your current state of health, as well as that of your employees, making a positive contribution to performance in your organization? Are you Fit to Lead? Are they Fit to Lead?

When the Fit to Lead program extends beyond yourself— when it becomes a contagious positive infection that affects your entire company—startling results begin to emerge. Numerous studies definitively show that when entire companies become Fit to Lead, absenteeism drops, productivity increases, and health-care costs plummet. Let's first look more closely at the Fit to Lead companywide benefits, and then discuss how you can get the same results at your company.

The Fit to Lead Corporation

More and more companies are now offering wellness and fitness programs to their employees. They are doing so because unfit and unhealthy workers hit companies where it hurts—in their pockets. Health-care costs have skyrocketed in recent years, and study after study shows that the only viable solution for keeping such costs down is creating a healthier workforce.

Not only is a fit workforce more productive and less likely to miss work for health reasons, a wealth of research has uncovered a direct link between the existence of company-sponsored fitness programs and lower health costs. According to some studies, a company can expect to save $153 per employee per year simply by implementing a wellness program. Those savings include fewer physician, hospital, and sick day expenditures.

Here are some compelling examples:

- Johnson & Johnson estimates that its employee health program, which encourages employees to exercise more and stop smoking, saved the company $1 million over five years.

- Florida Power and Light built twenty-seven fitness centers during the early '90s for its employees. They also posted wellness messages around their offices and offered additional health promotion programs. Result: They reduced health-care costs by 35 percent and worker compensation costs by 38 percent per claim.

- Prudential reported a 45 percent drop in health costs after starting a fitness program.

- A school district that adopted a fitness program saw a drop in teacher absenteeism by one day per teacher per year, resulting in an annual net savings of $150,000.

- Most companies report a return of $2 to $6 for every $1 they invest in employee health and fitness.

But it goes beyond the tangible. You compete with other companies for your best employees. When salary remains constant, the services you offer give you an edge—or not. As you now know, fit employees make better workers. To attract them to your company, you must offer fitness centers and programs.

However, to make fitness programs work, you need to do more than simply build a gym and place an OPEN sign on the door. For fitness to work, employees must embrace fitness, which brings us to the concept of SuperLeadership.

An important focus of this book is on effective leadership practice. Effective leadership is both an avenue for promoting health and fitness in others as well as an outcome of a healthier, more fit lifestyle. That means that living and being healthy is a critical path to becoming a more effective leader.

However, simply setting an example and even offering fitness programs may not be enough to bring your company from flabby to fit. You may need to encourage some employees one-on-one to take on the Fit to Lead program. Not everyone will enthusiastically embrace the concept.

Here is everything you need to know to inspire fitness in even the seemingly most uninspired employees.

What *Not* to Do

Imagine that you are a department manager in a medium-sized corporation. Ten people work in your department. James Bushel is one of these individuals. You were instrumental in his being hired a little over a year ago. You were impressed with his solid experience and especially the motivated attitude he seemed to display during his job interview.

Unfortunately, James has been creating some problems recently for a new health and fitness program that you have been coordinating for voluntary participants from the department. You still believe that Jim, in general, has the intelligence, ability, and motivation to be a very good organization member, but you feel that you need to address the difficulties he is currently posing for this program.

Specifically, your company has been advocating the benefits of a healthy lifestyle for all employees. In that spirit, your company has been encouraging different units to take advantage of ongoing fitness opportunities such as the various aerobics, strength-training, and other classes being offered through the company fitness center. In response to this companywide effort, you decided to work with the fitness center to create a three-day-a-week program called Fit to Lead that is specifically tailored to your department. Six of the department's ten employees agreed to participate along with you, and recently two others have expressed interest in joining the group.

To date the group has met for four weeks of forty-five-minute sessions consisting of moderate aerobic exercises, light strength training, and some practical nutritional counseling. Overall, the response from the group has been very positive. Some members have even begun to describe how much better they feel already and have reported various benefits such as weight loss, higher energy levels, and reduced stress.

James, however, has not responded well. This is disappointing, since James is generally a cooperative employee. Also, you feel that he could greatly benefit from the Fit to Lead program since he is noticeably overweight, smokes, and lives on a diet of mostly fast foods such as doughnuts, hot dogs, ice cream, and beer. Initially he seemed to be supportive of the program and was among the first to volunteer to participate. Unfortunately, shortly after the Fit to Lead sessions began, his enthusiasm seemed to fade. For the past few sessions especially, he has been late and has been participating halfheartedly at best.

You are concerned that James's negative attitude is going to rub off on other members of the group. You have overheard him criticizing the whole program on several occasions. You are convinced that the program is in fact significantly benefiting yourself and the others, and you have noticed a calmer, more relaxed yet productive atmosphere in your department that has contributed to noticeable performance improvements. At the same time it is clear that James is not motivated or committed to Fit to Lead and is detracting from the experience of others.

On three occasions you have reminded James that participation is voluntary and that he does not have to be involved, but each time he has said it is no problem and that he will continue. You realize that James's behavior has to change or he is going to drag down the efforts of the rest of the group. You have tried to give him time to adjust, but now a month has gone by and things are getting worse instead of better. You've decided that James requires some kind of special leadership attention from you, but you're not sure what to do.

Choose one of the three approaches listed below to deal with the situation and write down a couple of ideas regarding how you would use the strategy to deal with James.

1. Be more firm and direct with James. Use critical feedback and reprimands to get him either to change his behavior or drop out of the program.

2. Establish positive incentives for James. Use recognition and other rewards to improve his motivation to constructively participate.

3. Articulate your vision for the Fit to Lead program and how you think it can significantly benefit the department. Especially focus on how you view James fitting into that vision as a means of obtaining his commitment.

The case of James raises three of the most commonly used leadership approaches—and they all contain important flaws. The first choice suggests a directive, controlling approach. It involves getting James to behave the way you want him to, whether he likes it or not, and using your leadership authority to force or intimidate him to do it. The second choice focuses on an exchange relationship. Using the carrot (and sometimes the stick) in order to get followers to reach objectives is the key here. The third choice is based on providing an inspiring vision. You attempt to motivate James based on your positive vision for the Fit to Lead program.

Each choice can certainly serve as a way to lead others. However, they can all fail miserably because all three center on the leader. The leader is in the limelight and tends to do the thinking and make all the decisions. Consequently, followers can come to feel more like pawns on a giant chessboard without really caring deep down whether they do their best. Let's examine each of these common approaches to leadership in more detail to find out exactly where they can lead you astray.

Why Many Common Approaches
Fail to Inspire Fitness

Many people view leadership as a top-down process in which one person (a leader) influences another (a follower) to do something. Some leaders accomplish this through threat and intimidation stemming from their position of authority. This type of leadership is sometimes called the strongman approach, because it stems from the days of male-dominated leadership, often based on intimidation and punishment.

At other times, leaders use a transactional approach. For this method, a leader exchanges incentives and rewards for subordinate compliance. As with the strongman view, this type of leader is not concerned that followers like or believe in what they are doing.

Both of these approaches focus on leaders as the thinkers and followers as the means for the leaders to accomplish their ends. Followers comply with the leader's directions either in order to receive something of value (a reward) or in order to avoid something undesirable (a punishment). Followers often comply by doing the minimum that the leader asks.

Yet another leadership style centers on vision and inspiration. It calls for leaders to be "visionary heroes" and to create and communicate inspiring visions that motivate others to do what the leader sees as desirable. The leader motivates others to pursue the cause that has been spelled out in the leader's vision. As a result, followers can come to believe in the leader and/or the leader's cause.

This type of leadership can instill commitment in followers (rather than the limited compliance of the previous types of leadership). In return, followers typically go above and beyond the call of duty, willing to do more than the leader asks.

Sounds like the way to lead, right? Yet, again, this leadership style doesn't always add up to perfect results. The commitment that such leaders instill is usually limited to the leaders and/or their causes. When the leader isn't around, commitment usually drops off.

With each of the above types of leadership, the leader is the primary source of ideas and direction, and followers are the source of the effort and labor. So what happened to James? That all depends on the leadership choice you made. If you chose any of the three alternative leadership approaches listed, it is not likely that James would experience a long-term commitment to fitness or success with the Fit to Lead program. For that a different kind of leadership would be needed—SuperLeadership—an approach we describe later in the chapter.

The problem is that no one person can have all or even most of the answers. Even if it were realistic to expect persons in leadership positions to be able to provide the answers and directions and for followers simply to follow, we still would be faced with serious problems. Followers have a hard time getting excited about goals that they do not help shape and methods to reach the goals that they do not help to develop. And lifestyle decisions that affect health and fitness are issues over which most people especially want to exercise significant choice and influence.

Followers, just like leaders, want to feel that they are competent, significant, and valued persons in their organization. The reality is, with mounting competitive pressures from around the world, successful organizations need all employees to serve as valuable resources who share their knowledge and ideas, as well as their labor. Besides, it is important to remember that everyone is a leader. We all lead ourselves. Regardless of the influence and authority that people are subject to, in the end it is the individual who decides what to think and do, and whether to follow a leader. This means that being Fit to Lead is relevant to everyone.

Stop and reflect for a moment. When you have served in positions of leadership, to what extent do you believe you kept the spotlight focused on yourself and away from your followers? Write down some of your thoughts below.

_____

_____

_____

_____

_____

Despite their drawbacks, threat, reward, and vision can produce a kind of motivation to accomplish what the leader wants. This can potentially include exercise, diet, and other work and lifestyle changes. However, health and lifestyle are highly personal matters. If the inspiration, desire, and thinking for making lifestyle changes are centered in someone else (a leader), the person in question will have minimal ownership of the process. Consider the following story about Chris Tactum.

Chris was a critical employee for Maric Tech. He was the chief designer for new product development. Unfortunately, his long hours and high-stress work style had gradually created noticeable health problems for him. Over the two years that he worked in this position, Chris had gained about twenty-five pounds and found that the energy he had once enjoyed had declined significantly. He also became ill much more frequently, causing costly delays in some of Maric's new product releases, not to mention a great deal of frustration for Chris.

Alisa Clark, the corporate vice president and Chris's boss, tried to discuss this issue with him on several occasions. Alisa was an avid runner and a member of a fitness center that she visited at least twice a week for strength and flexibility training. She prided herself on her level of fitness and general health and high energy level. She tried to motivate Chris to take better care of his health.

At first she tried praising Chris when she noticed him making healthy choices such as drinking fruit juice at a break or walking the stairs instead of riding the elevator. A couple of times, when Chris had done a particularly nice job in his work, she even excused him from a meeting or paperwork, encouraging him to take a break and suggesting that he might go outside for a brisk walk.

When it was obvious that this positive approach was not having much effect, she decided to get more blunt with Chris. She let him know that she was disappointed in him when he had a project delay, even when she was aware that the delay was due to one of his recent illnesses. She also confronted him on his apparent lack of energy to keep up with the demands of his job.

Eventually she even tried to inspire him by verbally creating a positive mental image of all the benefits of being healthy and fit. But none of her motivational efforts worked. At this point she decided simply to address the issue with Chris in a heart-to-heart manner, trying to persuade him to make some healthy lifestyle changes.

"Chris, I know you don't think you have the time to make healthy work and lifestyle choices, but I wish you would make it a priority to pace yourself and get some exercise even during work hours. You are crucial to our company's future and we would rather you take an extra half hour at lunch for your health than try to rush back to log more hours. And your long hours, including late nights and weekends, just can't be good for you. As you know, I make it a priority to keep my work life balanced by working at a healthy pace and getting plenty of exercise, and I feel great—"

Chris cut her short in a tone that made it clear that he was not impressed. "I'm glad you are enjoying your healthy lifestyle, Alisa, but we are different people. Frankly, I consider my health and life choices to be personal. I appreciate your concern, but I am doing the best I can to survive the current pressures we face in the industry. Maybe sometime in the future, when things settle down, I'll have time to look into some lifestyle changes, but I can't right now. And frankly, I'm trying to get a report out to one of our project teams that is meeting later this afternoon, so I need to get back to work."

Over time, Alisa continued to encourage Chris to take better care of himself. Once she even convinced him to accompany her to her fitness center, but it did not go well. As she guided him through her usual exercise routine, she could tell that he was both uncomfortable and bored.

Alisa thought back on Chris's situation and concluded that there was not much more she could have done to help. Despite her good intentions, Chris simply could not identify with what she was encouraging him to do. He did not "own" the process.

Alisa was incorrect in concluding that she could do no more to inspire Chris to embrace fitness. Was there a better way to help Chris find the motivation to take more interest and responsibility for his health and fitness? Is there a better way to lead?

We believe there is. The answer lies in a concept called Super-Leadership, an approach that offers huge results when it comes to motivating employees to become Fit to Lead.

A Better Way to Lead

SuperLeadership meets the challenges of leading empowered employees and provides a powerful leadership alternative. It meets the kinds of challenges leaders face in our highly complex and rapidly changing world. SuperLeadership does not imply that leaders are supposed to be all-powerful, all-knowing, and capable of dealing with all problems on their own. On the contrary, SuperLeaders become super, with the strength of ten and more, because that strength is based on the talents, experience, and capability of others. SuperLeaders bring out the inner leadership—the self-leadership—of others.

According to SuperLeadership, effective leaders do not bend the wills of others to their own. Rather, they empower others to stand on their own two feet and to feel ownership of their job. SuperLeadership suggests that the spotlight should be on followers at least as much as leaders. In fact, the fundamental idea is to help employees to become SuperFollowers who are leaders in their own right—that is, leaders of themselves. This means that the leader's task becomes a process of helping employees to master self-leadership skills such as those described in Chapter 5. SuperLeadership includes seven specific steps that you can follow when you lead others.

Let's take a look at each of these steps, as well as how Alisa might have used them to inspire Chris to become Fit to Lead.

Seven Steps to SuperLeadership

Step 1. Become an effective self-leader. The first step to becoming a SuperLeader is becoming a better self-leader. The more effective you are in leading yourself toward fitness, the more likely others will follow in your footsteps.

Start by setting specific challenging but achievable goals for exercise and diet and then reward yourself for your progress and accomplishments. You can also redesign aspects of your own life and work to create a more healthy lifestyle while still meeting your responsibilities. For example, build in rest and stretch breaks to reduce stress and keep your body relaxed and vibrant. Also practice thinking constructively and positively with a focus on opportunities rather than retreating from obstacles. (For more ideas on how to be a more effective self-leader, see Chapter 5.)

Alisa has already largely accomplished this step by embarking on her own Fit to Lead journey and by mastering self-leadership. The key is that she needs to start with herself first. Once she is effectively leading herself to long-term health and fitness, she is in a more credible and better-informed position to help others.

Step 2. Model self-leadership for followers. Once you've mastered some self-leadership strategies yourself, vividly display these effective techniques for your followers to see and learn from. Demonstrate self-leadership strategies in a clear and credible manner, and give followers a chance to try them for themselves and to adapt them to their own needs. When others see you clearly introducing healthy practices into your daily routine and openly expressing the priority you place on them, they will have a live model to encourage them to consider their own health choices. Taking brisk walks as part of a lunch hour routine as well as choosing healthy foods when you dine together can communicate your commitment to health.

Alisa tried this step by bringing Chris to her fitness center, but this seemed to backfire. After some more thought, she decided not to give up so quickly. On her next attempt, Alisa asked Chris to join her for lunch. During the meal, she chose healthy yet flavorful foods. She also began taking short walks at lunch and inviting Chris to join her as they discussed business along the way. Soon Chris realized that problem solving and creativity can actually be stimulated by healthy activity and he began to understand why Alisa seemed to be so effective in her work.

Step 3. Encourage followers to set their own goals. Unless special attention is devoted to healthy lifestyle choices in the form of specific goals, it is very difficult consistently to follow through with practical exercise, diet, and other health-promoting practices. By helping followers learn the importance of setting significant but realistic targets for their health activities—for example, committing to taking a brisk twenty- to thirty-minute walk each day—the possibility for significant health benefits is greatly increased. First, you can help them set their goals, then gradually allow them to set goals for themselves.

Alisa largely accomplished this step through some simple conversations with Chris. During one, she asked Chris, "What do you feel like you might want to work toward right now in terms of your fitness? Can you think of a specific goal, such as losing ten pounds in the next six months or working up to running three miles without stopping?"

Chris responded, "I haven't really thought about it. I'd just like to be in better shape."

Alisa followed up, "What do you mean by getting in shape? What would that look like in three to six months?"

Eventually Chris got the idea and set some meaningful goals that fit his own specific needs.

Step 4. Create positive thought patterns. Help followers to see their own potential and capabilities for being fit and healthy. Help them to believe in themselves. Also, encourage them to look for the opportunities nested in their daily challenges rather than focusing on all the reasons to give up and stop trying. Much of success or failure in progressing toward a healthier life depends on the way we think about this in our minds. Every slip—an extra piece of cake or failing to perform a daily exercise routine—can provide the opportunity for exploring how a fitness-focused self-leadership program can be further improved for future success.

Alisa asked Chris how he felt about his previous attempts to get in better shape. They talked through how what he learned from those past failed attempts could provide him with new alternatives and opportunities for success in the future. Chris already knew some things that hadn't worked, so he decided not to include those things in his future efforts. He had also discovered some strategies that seemed to work for a while and that, with some adjustments, he thought could be successful in the long run. One of the key ones was performing activities that he naturally enjoyed. For example, he really liked hiking in nature settings and often forgot that he was ex-

ercising at all. Later, hiking (especially with friends) would become an important part of his fitness activities.

Step 5. Reward self-leadership (and promote constructive critical feedback). Recognize and reward followers for initiative, taking on responsibility, and using self-leadership strategies that promote their health, fitness, and subsequent performance. The focus of praise should shift to effective self-leadership rather than just performance. Also, as followers become more confident, they will be better able to accept constructive critical feedback on how they can further improve. The key is that the feedback should be constructive. And over time, the follower should develop the ability to provide his or her own constructive feedback for a long-term Fit to Lead lifestyle.

Alisa praised Chris when she saw him making healthy choices on his own, such as planning an upcoming hike that he offered to lead several of his coworkers on. She also did this when she observed him trying to come up with strategies to keep himself on track to better fitness, such as recording exercise sessions on his calendar or writing short-term goals into his daily planner.

Step 6. Promote self-leading teamwork. Encouraging followers to work together and help one another is also very important. When people commit to exercising together and encouraging and reinforcing one another for making healthy life choices, success is frequently improved significantly. Teams are a crucial part of effective worker empowerment. If individuals choose to work as a team on their health practices, a solid foundation for a Fit to Lead organization can be established.

Alisa encouraged Chris to try exercising with friends or coworkers, and for them to support one another. Soon Chris was making more frequent healthy choices that he was able to enjoy in the company of those he liked spending time with. On some occasions (such as in regard to the upcoming hike he was going to lead), Alisa even began to notice Chris encouraging others to get some exercise with him or to eat more healthily at lunch.

Step 7. Facilitate a self-leadership culture. Work to establish values and norms that center on health and fitness initiative and self-leadership. If the first six steps are carried out effectively, this process should unfold naturally. In general, encourage, guide, and reward healthy self-leadership behavior while continually demonstrating in your own actions effective self-leadership that promotes long-term Fit to Lead health.

Interestingly, over time Chris actually became an important source of inspiration for health and fitness to others in the organization. His discovery of the joys of nature hiking branched out into biking and cross-country skiing, and it was not unusual for Chris to be an organizer of healthy employee outings on weekends. And when you added in all the other unique health interests of many other employees who enjoyed the value and priority placed on fitness by Alisa and other executives in their organization (and who supported it with resources and positive recognition), over time the organization truly became a Fit to Lead place to work.

We specifically developed the SuperLeadership approach to fit with the challenges of contemporary leadership in a complex and rapidly changing world. The SuperLeader leads others to lead themselves. In many challenging situations, SuperLeadership can be used to help others with their health and fitness activities. In fact, SuperLeadership can be the critical component for establishing a comprehensive Fit to Lead culture throughout an organization. By serving as an example and encouraging and reinforcing followers for taking responsibility, initiative, and working effectively with others for their own health and fitness, a leader can become a Super-Leader. Fit to Lead SuperLeaders lead others to be Fit to Lead themselves.

Take a moment to reflect again. Have you ever served as a Super-Leader for others? Your coworkers? Your children or other relatives? Consider writing down some of your thoughts on how and when you did this.

How might you use SuperLeadership to help others to lead themselves to a healthier "fit to lead themselves" lifestyle? How might SuperLeadership be used to help others such as James and Chris discussed earlier in this chapter?

Study the seven steps of SuperLeadership. Which of the steps have you used effectively in the past? Which steps do you need to work on to be able to use them more effectively for promoting health and fitness in those you lead?

"I've been following the principles of the Fit to Lead program for at least fifteen years now. Due to adhering to this regimen, I feel better, am more creative, have more energy, and am much more productive than I ever imagined. Exercise and the right diet have made a positive impact on my approach to business as well as my personal life. The *Fit to Lead* message is not just talk. The program works."

—Sherry Ann Petta, president and founder,

Especially Specialties, Inc.

Notes

Introduction

1. The quotations here and elsewhere by Michael Mangum, Tom Monaghan, and James Harris are from personal interviews conducted by Christopher Neck on February 26, 1999 (Mangum), March 23, 1999 (Monaghan), and March 15, 1999 (Harris). The other executive fitness examples are from D. Jones, "Many Successful Women Are Also Athletic," *USA Today,* March 26, 2002, p. 1B; K. Hannon, "Profile: Charles Rossotti," *USA Today,* February 17, 1999, p. 7B; A.J. Michels, "Doctor's Orders: CEOs of Pharmaceutical Companies Stay Fit Through Exercise and a Healthy Diet," *Fortune* 125, no. 12 (June 15, 1992): 13–15; S. Kilman, "Sears Names as Chief Financial Officer Day, Who Helped Revive Safeway Inc.," *The Wall Street Journal,* March 5, 1999, p. B-8.

2. For details related to this survey, see J. Leinfelder, "Executive Training: How Five Managers Keep That Lean and Hungry Look," *Corporate Report—Minnesota,* 22, no. 5 (1991): 86–93; J.M. Rippe, "CEO Fitness: The Performance Plus," *Psychology Today* 23, no. 5 (1989): 50–54.

3. Unless otherwise indicated, information about George W. Bush and other top executives is from personal interviews conducted by the author team.

Chapter One. Why Should You Get Fit?

1. Some of the material in this chapter was adapted from and inspired by C. P. Neck and K. H. Cooper, "The Fit Executive: Exercise and Diet Guidelines for Enhanced Performance," *Academy of Management Executive* 14, no. 2 (2000): 72–83.

2. The quotations by Judith Kaplan and Carol Cone are from Rippe, "CEO Fitness."

3. For more information on these studies and others that examine the fitness-performance relationship, see R.J. Shephard, "Do Work-Site Exercise and Health Programs Work?" *The Physician and Sports Medicine* 27 (1999): 48–72; D.R. Frew and N.S. Bruning, "Improved Productivity and Job Satisfaction Through Employee Exercise Programs," *Hospital Material Management Quarterly* 9 (1988): 62–69;

L. R. Gettman, "The Effect of Employee Physical Fitness on Job Performance," *Personnel Administrator* (November 1980): 41–61.

4. For a discussion of these and other studies focusing on fitness–mental performance, see N. S. Lupinacci et al., "Age and Physical Activity Effects on Reaction Time and Digit Symbol Substitution Performance in Cognitively Active Adults," *Research Quarterly for Exercise and Sport* 64, no. 2 (1993): 144–51; D. J. Bunce, A. Barrowclough, and I. Morris, "The Moderating Influence of Physical Fitness on Age Gradients in Vigilance and Serial Choice Responding Tasks," *Psychology and Aging* 11, no. 4 (1996): 671–82; J. C. Wojtek et al., "The Influence of Physical Fitness on Automatic and Effortful Memory Changes in Aging," *International Journal of Aging and Human Development* 35, no. 4 (1992): 265–86.

5. For more discussion of the benefits of being fit, see K. H. Cooper, *It's Better to Believe* (Nashville: Thomas Nelson, 1995).

6. For an in-depth discussion of research on physical activity and psychological outcomes, see "Physical Activity and Psychological Benefits: Internal Society of Sport Psychology Position Statement," *The Physician and Sports Medicine* 20, no. 10 (1992): 179–84; J. E. Brandon and J. M. Loftin, "Relationship of Fitness to Depression, State and Trait Anxiety, Internal Health Locus of Control, and Self-Control," *Perceptual and Motor Skills* 73, no. 2 (1991): 563–66.

7. These remarks appear in Rippe, "CEO Fitness."

8. See A. M. Paolone et al., "Results of Two Years of Exercise Training in Middle-Aged Men," *The Physician and Sports Medicine* (December 1976): 77; D. Ornish et al., "Can Lifestyle Changes Reverse Coronary Heart Disease?" *Lancet* 336, no. 21 (July 1990): 129–33; Smolin, L. A., and Grossvenor, M. B., 1997. *Nutrition: Science and Applications,* 2nd Edition. Fort Worth: Saunders College Publishing. 354.

9. Department of Health and Human Services, "Healthy People 2000: National Health Promotion and Disease Prevention Objectives" (Washington, DC: 1990).

10. For a more precise discussion of these landmark studies, see E. E. Calle et al., "Body-Mass Index and Mortality in a Prospective Cohort of U.S. Adults," *The New England Journal of Medicine* 341 (1999): 1097–1105; S. N. Blair et al., "Physical Fitness and All-Cause Mortality: A Prospective Study of Healthy Men and Women," *Journal of the American Medical Association* 262, no. 17 (1989): 2395–401; S. N. Blair et al., "Changes in Physical Fitness and All-Cause Mortality: A Prospective Study of Healthy and Unhealthy Men," *Journal of the American Medical Association* 273, no. 14 (1995): 1093–98.

11. C. Romano, "In Sickness and in Health," *Management Review* 83, no. 5 (1994): 40–46.

12. See R. Ahrens, "The Healthy Workplace," *Inc.* 17, no. 11 (1995): 77–86.

13. "Economic Cost of Cardiovascular Diseases," American Heart Association Web site (americanheart.org/statistics/10econom.html).

14. National Heart, Lung, and Blood Institute, Department of Health and Human Services, Public Health Service, National Institutes of Health, *Cardiovascular Primer for the Workplace,* NIH publication 81-2210 (Washington, DC, 1981).

15. C. Hymovitz, "Need to Boost Morale?" *The Wall Street Journal,* May 28, 2002, p. B1.

16. Unless otherwise stated, the main sources for the prescriptions and other materials are the author team's own clinical testing and research.

Chapter Two. The Fit to Lead Prescription

1. The source of some of the information in this chapter is the Cooper Aerobics Center Web site (www.cooper-aerobics.com).

Chapter Three. No More Excuses

1. Cooper, *It's Better to Believe.*

2. See M. B. Higginbotham et al., "Physiologic Basis for the Age-Related Decline in Aerobic Work Capacity," *American Journal of Cardiology* 57 (1986): 1374–79; Cooper, *It's Better to Believe.*

3. For in-depth discussion of these studies and others that focus on the aerobic capacities of older people, see Cooper, *It's Better to Believe;* P. Haber, M. K. Honiger, and M. Niederberger, "Effects on Elderly People 67–76 Years of Age of Three-Month Endurance Training on a Bicycle Ergometer," *European Heart Journal* 5, Supplement E (1984): 37–39; J. Strovas, "Chronic Illness Need Not Deter Elderly Exercisers," *The Physician and Sports Medicine* 18, no. 2 (1990): 20.

4. For more discussion on aging and muscle mass decreases, see S. H. Cohen et al., "Compartmental Body Composition Based on the Body, Nitrogen, Potassium, and Calcium," *American Journal of Physiology* 239 (1980): 192–200; W. J. Evans and W. W. Campbell, "Sarcopenia and Age-Related Changes in the Body Composition and Functional Capacity," *Journal of Nutrition* 123 (1993): 465–68.

5. M. A. Fiatarone et al., "High-Intensity Strength Training in Nonagenarians," *Journal of the American Medical Association* 263, no. 22 (1990): 3029–34.

6. See R. R. Pate et al., "Physical Activity and Health: A Recommendation from The Centers for Disease Control and Prevention and

the American College of Sports Medicine," *Journal of the American Medical Association* 273, no. 5 (1995): 402–07.

7. See Blair, "Physical Fitness and All-Cause Mortality."

8. For insights into this Danish study and more information on the importance of muscle mass loss, see K. Hjort Sorensen, "State of Health and Its Association with Death Among Old People at Three-Years Follow-Up," Institute for Almen Medicine, Kobenhavns Universitet, Juliane Maries Vej 18, DK-2100 Kobenhavn O; Cooper, *It's Better to Believe.*

9. For a specific delineation of the relation of strength and bone loss, see M. Sinaki, "Exercise and Osteoporosis," *Archives of Physical Medicine and Rehabilitation* 70 (March 1989): 220–29; J. A. Work, "Strength Training: A Bridge to Independence for the Elderly," *The Physician and Sports Medicine* 17, no. 11 (1989): 134–38.

Chapter Four. Eating for Fitness

1. Research studies examining the link between fat intake and/or cholesterol levels and negative health outcomes include J. T. Dwyer, "Diet and Nutritional Strategies for Cancer Risk Reduction," *Cancer* 72 (1993): 1025–31; C. E. De Vries and C. J. van Noorden, "Effects of Dietary Fatty Acid Composition on Tumor Growth and Metastasis," *Anticancer Research* 12 (1992): 1513–22.

2. K. H. Cooper, *Nutritional Therapies* (Nashville: Thomas Nelson, Inc. 1996); Cooper, *It's Better to Believe.*

3. For other discussions on the relationship between fiber and health, see Council on Scientific Affairs, "Dietary Fiber and Health," *Journal of the American Medical Association* 262, no. 4 (1989): 542–46; B. O. Schneeman and J. Tietyen, "Dietary Fiber," in M. E. Shils, J. A. Olson, and M. Shike, eds., *Modern Nutrition in Health and Disease,* 8th ed. (Philadelphia: Lea & Febiger, 1994).

4. For further examination of the link between calcium intake and health, see R. Marcus, "Calcium Intake and Skeletal Integrity: Is There a Critical Relationship?" *The Journal of Nutrition* 117, no. 17 (1986): 631; G. Toss, "Effect of Calcium Intake and Other Lifestyle Factors in Bone Loss," *Journal of International Medical Research* 231 (1992): 181–86; V. W. Bunker, "The Role of Nutrition in Osteoporosis," *British Journal of Biomedical Science* 51 (1994): 228–40.

5. A primary source for our discussion on free radicals and antioxidants is *American Journal of Clinical Nutrition* 53, no. 1 (January 1991): 189S–396S.

6. For research findings and/or discussions supporting the relationship between free radical damage and negative health outcomes,

see C. G. Cochrane, "Cellular Injury by Oxidants," *The American Journal of Medicine,* Supplement 3C (September 1991): 303C–23Sff.; M. M. Kanter, "Free Radicals, Exercise, and Antioxidant Supplementation," *International Journal of Sport Nutrition* 4, no. 3 (1994): 205–25.

7. See K. H. Cooper, *Dr. Kenneth H. Cooper's Antioxidant Revolution* (Nashville: Thomas Nelson, 1994).

8. Comprehensive guidelines for optimal antioxidant dosages have been issued by the Cooper Clinic. For example, adults over the age of twenty-two should consume the following daily: vitamin C (1,000 mg), vitamin E (400 IU), beta-carotene (5,000 IU), folic acid (800 mcg), vitamin B$_6$ (50 mg), vitamin B$_{12}$ (400 mcg), and selenium (100 mcg). For other specific recommendations for optimal dosages of antioxidants, see Cooper, *Antioxidant Revolution.*

Chapter Five. Fit from the Inside Out

1. A portion of the material in this chapter was adapted from ideas in C. C. Manz and C. P. Neck, *Mastering Self-Leadership: Empowering Yourself for Personal Excellence,* 3rd Edition (Englewood Cliffs, NJ: Prentice-Hall, 2004); C. P. Neck et al., "Fit to Lead: Is Fitness the Key to Effective Executive Leadership?" *Journal of Managerial Psychology* 15, no. 8 (2000): 833–40; C. C. Manz, C. P. Neck, J. Mancuso, and K. Manz, *For Team Members Only: Making Your Workplace Team Productive and Hassle-Free* (New York: AMACOM, 1997).

2. P. E. Butler, *Talking to Yourself: Learning the Language of Self-Support* (San Francisco: Harper, 1981).

3. Carolyn White, "Sharpening Mental Skills: Athletes Embrace What Could Be Performance Revolution of '90s," *USA Today,* August 8, 1996.

4. David Burns, *Feeling Good: The New Mood Therapy* (New York: Morrow, 1980).

Chapter Seven. Your Total Life Makeover

1. For specifics on this two-part strength test and a complete scoring guide, see Cooper, *It's Better to Believe,* p. 47.

2. For specifics on this basic flexibility test and a complete scoring guide, see ibid., p. 50.

Chapter Eight. Becoming a SuperLeader

1. Some of the content in this chapter was inspired by and partly based on material from Manz, Neck, Mancuso, and Manz, *For Team*

Members Only. For more information on SuperLeadership, see Charles C. Manz and Henry P. Sims, Jr., *SuperLeadership* (New York: Berkley, 1990), and Charles C. Manz and Henry P. Sims, Jr., *The New Super-Leadership* (San Francisco: Berrett-Koehler, 2001).

About the Authors

Christopher P. Neck, Ph.D., an associate professor of management at Virginia Polytechnic Institute and State University, is a recognized authority on management and self-leadership. **Tedd L. Mitchell, M.D.**, is medical director for the Cooper Wellness Program at the Cooper Aerobics Center in Dallas, Texas. In June 2002, President George W. Bush appointed him to serve on the President's Council on Physical Fitness and Sports. **Charles C. Manz, Ph.D.**, holds the Charles and Janet Nirenberg Chair of Business Leadership in the Isenberg School of Management at the University of Massachusetts. He is a speaker, consultant, and bestselling author. **Emmet C. Thompson II, D.S.L.**, was a member of the fitness staff at the Cooper Fitness Center, where for six years he was head martial arts instructor and a personal trainer. He is now the executive director of the Fit to Lead Institute of the Cooper Aerobics Center Wellness Program. All of the authors stay fit by running, swimming, and performing various other athletic pursuits.